DATE DUE

DEMCO 38-296

敦煌藝術精華

THE CREAM OF DUNHUANG ART

敦煌芸術の粋

敦煌研究院編著

責任編輯　朱蔚英　鍾美玲
攝影　　　孫志軍
英文翻譯　郁雋明　寧強　純一
日文翻譯　朱洪江　鍾美玲
封面設計　趙俊榮
版式設計　梁梁
出版　　　香港廣彙貿易有限公司
總發行　　中國圖書進出口總公司
　　　　　中國北京朝陽區工體東路16號
印刷　　　中華商務彩色印刷有限公司
版次　　　1996年第3版
　　　　　ISBN 962-331-007-X

The Cream of Dunhuang Art

Edit	Dunhuang Research Academy
Editor in Chief	Duan Wenjie
Editor	Liang Weiying, Zhong Meiling
Photographer	Sun Zhijun
English Translator	Yu Junming, Ning Qiang, Chun Yi
Japanese Translator	Zhong Meiling
Designer if Cover	Zhao Jiang
Publisher	Polyspring Co., Ltd.
Distributor	China National Publications
	Import and Export Corporation
	16 Gongti East Road Beijing China
Printer	C & C Joint Printing Co., (HK) Ltd.
	Third Publised 1996
	ISBN 962-331-007-X

敦煌芸術の精華

編著　　　　敦煌研究院
監修者　　　段文傑
編集代表　　梁尉英　鍾美玲
撮影者　　　孫志軍
英文翻訳者　郁雋明　寧　強　純　一
和文翻訳者　朱洪江　鍾美玲
カバー設計　趙俊栄
レイ・アウト　梁　梁
出版者　　　香港広彙貿易有限公司
総販売会社　中国図書進出口総公司
　　　　　　中国北京朝陽区工體東路16号
印刷所　　　中華商務彩色印刷有限公司
版次　　　　1996年第3版発行
　　　　　　ISBN 962-331-007-X

内容提要

本畫册收載敦煌藝術中的壁畫、彩塑、絹畫、磚畫，書法精品136幅，並有專題論述和簡要的圖版說明，熔學術性、資料性於一體，既可瞭解與欣賞敦煌藝術，又可作爲研究資料。

ABSTRACT

This picture-album offers you 136 masterpieces of the mural paintings, painted sculptures, silk-paintings, brick-paintings and calligraphies in Dunhuang art, adding an academic thesis and the simple explanations of the plates. Through this combination of learning and material, you can not only understand and appreciate Dunhuang art, but also use it as research materials.

あらすじ

本写真集には敦煌芸術中の壁画、カラー彫塑、絹画、れんが画、書道など合計136件が収められてあると同時に、特定のテーマについての論述及び簡単で要領を得た図版の説明などが載せられてあるので、敦煌芸術が楽しまれる一方、研究資料にもなる。

目錄　CONTENTS　目次

圖版目錄

図版目録

輝煌燦爛的敦煌藝術

段文傑

（一）

敦煌藝術是產生和積存在敦煌的多門類的藝術綜合體，不僅僅指敦煌壁畫和敦煌彩塑，還包括敦煌建築、敦煌絹畫、敦煌版畫、敦煌書法、敦煌舞樂和敦煌染織、刺繡等工藝美術。廣義地講，還應包括敦煌文學、變文、曲辭等與壁畫有直接關係者。

敦煌藝術是宗教藝術。宗教是歷史的產物，它伴隨着人類發展的歷程而發展，從原始人類的自然宗教到人類分化爲階級之後的發展成熟的宗教，都與藝術結下了不解之緣。宗教需要藝術作宣傳，藝術依靠宗教而發展。我國遠古時代的圖騰形象，史前陶盆中的人面魚，晚周帛畫上的龍鳳鬥與婦人祈禱，戰國帛畫上的仙人御龍昇天，馬王堆西漢帛畫上導引死者靈魂昇天的圖像，顧愷之的《洛神賦》圖，酒泉丁家閘十六國墓畫中的東王公、西王母等等，都與宗教思想聯在一起，但它們都是我國美術史上的瑰寶。

從西方來看，兩萬年前的法國拉斯科洞窟壁畫中的野牛和鳥首人，兩千多年前的希臘奧陵比斯山上的諸神，天神宙斯、日神阿波羅、戰神阿瑞斯、智慧女神雅典娜，直到文藝復興時期羅馬教堂裡的壁畫，米開郎基羅的《創世紀》、達芬奇的《最後晚餐》，等等，都是宗教藝術，而且是舉世公認的西方藝術不可超越的典範。

敦煌藝術，是佛教題材的藝術。以莫高窟爲中心的敦煌石窟，上起十六國、下迄元、清，歷時千餘年，現存洞窟570多個，壁畫五萬多平方米，帛畫近千幅，彩塑近三千身，寫本三四萬件，織染刺繡一批。作爲我國的民族藝術瑰寶，都具有高度的歷史價值和藝術價值，都是稀世之珍，不愧爲我國的民族藝術珍寶和人類文化遺產的明珠。

（二）

從反映現實生活而言，敦煌藝術和世俗藝術一樣是一面歷史的鏡子。從壁畫和絹畫中可以看到不同時代、不同民族、不同階層各種各樣的事物，如勞動生產、歌舞昇平、悲歡離合、風土人情以及人的歷史命運。

在敦煌壁畫中有很多奔波於絲綢之路的中西商隊，其中420窟的商隊最爲生動。描寫商主乘馬率領着滿載絲綢的毛驢隊、駱駝隊西行。途中駱駝臥病，行人立刻診治灌藥。毛驢負重，險路難行，上山時前拉後推，下山時抓住尾巴，不小心駱駝滾下了山坡，貨物掉進了水塘。駄夫摔倒在懸崖，爬起來，拾起貨物，捆在另一駱駝上繼續前行；轉過山谷，强盜攔路搶劫，一場惡戰之後，貨物被洗劫一空。這幅畫眞實地反映了漢唐以來絲綢之路的艱難險阻。在這遼闊漫長的絲綢之路上"切稅商胡以斷行旅"是不足爲奇的。北周時，涼州刺史攔劫胡商；初唐時，玄奘在中亞遇盜；晚唐時，回鶻人攔劫中朝天使，等等，不一而足。

初唐220窟貞觀十六年的《帝王出行圖》，是早於當時官居右相的著名畫家閻立本的《歷代帝王圖》的傑作，描寫漢族帝王盛裝出行，着大襦，前有侍者張羽扇，障蔽風塵，後有大臣扶持。大臣冠上插貂尾，手持文卷，是相當於宰相一級大臣的標誌。大臣後有一組各民族君長，戴氈帽、皮帽，着圓領窄袖胡服，拱手而立，這是帝王圖中的新內容。據歷史記載，唐太宗實行"愛之如一"的民族政策之後，到長安朝廷做官的各族首領達百人之多。外出巡幸，"四夷君長咸從"。武則天封泰山也是這樣，突厥、波斯、于闐、罽賓等十餘國君長隨行。

榆林窟吐蕃時期的第25窟《彌勒變》中的嫁娶圖，畫靑廬（帳房）中舉行婚禮的場面，帳中設長案，置果品，男女賓客，蕃漢併坐，圍屏內新郎新娘正在賓相陪侍下行跪拜禮，五體投地的新郎是吐蕃族，鳳冠披帛的新娘是漢族。這幅漢蕃聯姻圖是象徵性的，但它的影子則是文成公主入藏、金城公主和蕃。

盛唐454窟《彌勒變》中的耕獲圖。是根據佛經"一種七收"一語而作，一開始便是"二牛抬槓"，農夫手把曲轅犁耕地播種，接着是收割、打場、揚場，糧食成堆，斗斛橫呈。地邊農婦送來飲水和飯菜，饑渴的農夫抱着水罐仰面痛飲。在廳堂裡坐着紅袍官吏（或地主），農夫長跪稟報，這豈不是一幅生動的收租圖嗎？這幅畫還說明曲轅犁已從中原傳到了邊疆。

敦煌壁畫中，舞樂場面很多，主要有天樂和俗樂。天樂指天人形象出現於佛國世界的舞樂，俗樂指世俗生活畫面中的舞樂。流行於河西的主要是西涼樂。所謂西涼樂，就是西域各民族的舞樂，主要是龜茲樂加上外來的天竺樂，與中原舞樂相結合的舞樂。北朝溫子昇所說的"敦煌樂"，大概就是這樣一個多種成份結合的舞樂。就壁畫中的樂器看，有中原樂器，如箏、簫（排簫）、方響、笙、阮咸等；有西域民族樂器，如腰鼓、齊鼓、答臘鼓、雞婁鼓、五弦、篳篥等；也有外國傳來的樂器，如琵琶、箜篌、銅鈸等。從舞蹈看，有中原舞，悠揚婉轉，揮袖而舞，所謂"長袖善舞"正是中原舞的特點。唐代《宋國夫人出行圖》中的四女伎，高髻衫裙，披帛長袖，翩翩起

舞，唐人贊揚清商伎的詩中寫道：“妙手輕回拂長袖，高歌浩唱發淸音。”有西域舞，西域民族性格爽朗，感情激揚，歌舞節奏强烈。如220窟在西域燈輪光影下的兩組舞蹈，一組戴寶冠，着錦半臂，腰束石榴裙，作男裝；一組披髮，裸體，白練裙，髮絡飄揚，作女裝。都在小圓毯子上縱橫騰踏，揮舞紅巾，旋轉如風。這就是元稹《胡旋女》詩中所謂“驪珠迸珥逐飛星，虹暈輕巾掣流電”的西域胡舞。

敦煌藝術中蘊藏的歷史是豐富多彩的，它是以漢族爲主體的多民族聚居的國際絲綢市場和中西文化交流的國際都會歷史變遷的一面鏡子。

（三）

敦煌藝術和其他藝術一樣，都是創造美的，許多優秀作品以其强烈的藝術魅力吸引着人們，通過審美享受，在潛移默化中發揮宗教宣傳作用。

敦煌藝術的美也是多種多樣的。

敦煌彩塑，和所有佛敎雕塑一樣，借用眞實的人物形象，象徵神靈的智慧和力量，象徵善艮美好的願望。

佛陀以莊嚴慈祥的巨像，象徵品德圓滿、至高無上的聖者複雜抽象的內涵。北魏的禪定佛像，結跏安坐，嫣然含笑，象徵超脫塵世、忘懷萬慮的禪悅之樂；唐代魁武的天王，揮戈持劍，脚踏惡鬼，象徵天國的安寧；宮娃般妍麗嫻雅的唐代菩薩，象徵大慈大悲、濟世活人的品德，而菩薩的女性化則反映了美的中國特色。

敦煌絹畫，指藏經洞發現的絹本和紙本畫，目前已知者達七八百幅之多，內容十分豐富，有各種經變、佛菩薩像、佛教史迹畫、供養人畫像和裝飾圖案等類。由於在庫房裡存放了近千年，殘損較甚，但多數形象淸晰，色彩格外鮮麗，這批被劫瑰寶與石窟壁畫同樣珍貴。

如《樹下說法圖》是初唐傑作，畫釋迦結跏坐樹下，身着通肩朱紅袈裟，作說法狀；兩側四菩薩各有姿態，濃黑的垂髮，襯托出紅潤的肢體和面龐，透明的巾帔虛無縹渺，增强了宗教的神秘感。身後六個弟子，形象各異，而表情則同，在和顏悅色中，透露出爽朗的心境。寶座下的女供養人，椎髻，窄袖衫裙，雙手持蓮，長跪供養，沉靜而閑暢。它與329窟說法圖中的女供養人幾乎相同，均爲高手之作。

這幅說法圖以封閉式構圖，表現了莊嚴靜穆而溫婉愉悅的神秘境界。

又如引路菩薩，是一位具有女性美的鬚眉男子，菩薩乘紫雲，左手持紅蓮白幡，引導亡靈，右手持香爐，香烟裊裊上昇，烟霧迷濛中出現一座宮殿樓閣——幻想中的天國，菩薩回首顧盼，似乎正在爲紫雲中的亡靈指示去路。小小的靈魂是一位豪華貴婦人，頭飾抛家髻，身穿大袖襦，造型與周昉的簪花仕女相同，拱手胸前，默默地跟着菩薩走去。充分表現了引向天國之路的主題思想，創造了紫氣瀰漫的自然空間，與亡靈之間的冥冥和諧的意境美。

敦煌書法，指藏經洞發現的數萬件漢文寫本，保存着兩晉南北朝直到宋代的各種書法。這是一大批民間書法藝術珍品，其中寫經體和楷書頗多精品。

早期的寫經體，是在漢簡書法草隸基礎上發展起來的過渡到楷書的中間形態。多出自敦煌書法家之手，如晉的索靖，北魏令狐崇哲、曹法壽等。書前先畫烏絲欄，使寫本嚴整統一，字形結構一如隸書，落筆運力則與隸書不同，往往橫道落筆輕而細，收筆用頓力，字形豐肥圓潤，結體凝重，行氣暢展，別具風格，表現了童稚天眞之美。

隋唐楷書則多傳自中原，且多爲長安朝廷門下省和弘文館書手之作。僧智永、弘文館學士歐陽詢的楷書在敦煌頗爲流行，結體規整，筆力遒勁，表現了隋唐楷書圓潤典雅之美。

敦煌版畫，在初盛唐時期已經出現，木版單綫雕刻，墨色刷印，亦有刷印後上色者，如初盛唐時期的游戲座觀音菩薩，晚唐咸通九年（868年）的《金剛經》插圖《祇樹給孤獨園圖》，五代開運四年（947年）曹元忠施北方毗沙門天王像等。特別是《祇樹給孤獨園圖》，釋迦牟尼側面說法，十大弟子、釋梵天王、金剛力士簇擁左右，座下佛弟子長跪。此圖結構活潑，刻工精細。綫條是造型的唯一藝術語言，綫刻技術已達到高度純熟的境地，通體鐵綫，挺拔有力，黑白相襯，疏密有致，人物雖小而栩栩如生，充分表現了綫如曲鐵盤絲的力感美。

內容美。有人說，敦煌壁畫內容，說神道鬼，離奇荒誕。古人早有批評。但故事多來自公元前成書的《本生經》，有許多印度民間寓言故事，內容健康優美。

如《九色鹿本生》，描寫九色鹿不顧自身安危跳入急流，拯救溺人，而溺人見利忘義，出賣了九色鹿，在遭到國王大兵團團圍困時，九色鹿臨危不懼，堅持正義，斥責溺人忘恩負義，與邪惡作堅決的鬥爭，表現高尚的道德品格美。

《象護與金象》的故事，描寫象護出生時出現一金象，他們形影不離，同時長大。金象

大小便落地成金，因而家中黃金滿庫。象護長大入學，一次同學們講述各家奇聞，象護即講述金象的故事。同學中有一位王子，聽後心中暗思，我如果做了國王一定要將金象奪取過來。於是設計殺害了父母，篡奪了王位，立即派人邀請象護父子乘象入宮赴宴，受到國王隆重款待。象護想，國王一向貪暴，突然如此殷勤，必有詭計，即向國王辭行。國王說：人可以走，金象留下。象護父子恍然大悟，即空步出宮。國王手撫金象，十分得意，忽然金象沒入地下，又在宮外出現，正好在象護父子面前，父子二人跨上象背奔回家中，使國王的鴻門宴落了一場空，表現了諷刺性寓言故事之美。

其他如《張騫出使西域》、《張議潮統軍出行》都是歷史人物畫，表現英雄人物愛國思想。

敦煌藝術內容豐富而複雜，其中有優美的，也有醜惡的。但美的善的，體現中國美學思想的美與善結合是主要的。

形式美。藝術的內容必須有完美的形式來表現，通過美的形式，激發觀者的審美感情。敦煌藝術的形式有多種層次。外形式，如每個洞窟結構的立體形式，上有藻井懸華蓋，象徵天空；四壁畫神靈形象，作巨型經變以示極樂幻景；正龕設佛陀及侍從，象徵佛國世界的主宰者；地面鋪蓮磚，象徵淨土，人們進入洞，猶如化生佛國。這就是一個以建築、雕塑和壁畫等藝術作品組合起來的、人間世界不存在的包含着追求人生真諦的複雜內涵的外形式。

每幅畫也有適應內容的外形式。單幅畫，表達單一主題的形式；組畫，表達多種主題的聯合形式；連續式，表現不同時間、空間和曲折情節的橫卷式或立軸式；三聯式，即三位一體式，在主題畫兩側安排對聯式的故事畫，這些外形式都是適應內容需要的民族繪畫形式的新發展。

內形式，指體現主題思想在畫面上的內容結構。內形式也多種多樣。有順序式，按故事的發生、發展、高潮、結束規律，順序鋪陳。如佛傳故事，從乘象入胎到成道說法，一生事迹，脈絡分明。有衝突式，故事從兩頭開始，在畫面中部矛盾衝突的高潮中結束，如《九色鹿本生》、《睒子本生》等。有高潮式，故事一開始便展現衝突的高潮，然後逐漸降低調子，《五百強盜成佛》便是如此。有眾星拱月式，主體畫面四周，環繞穿插各種故事，形成向心型結構，巨型經變多屬此類。有雙主體式，兩個主體人物遙遙相對，神通變化展現其間，《維摩變》、《勞度叉鬥聖變》均屬此類。有自由式，故事情節隨意佈置，或往返進行，或左右穿插，沒有規律，經變中穿插故事，屏風畫多屬此類。

內形式的要求是創造空間境界，即意境，大多體現在巨型經變中，基本可分為兩類構圖。一類是開放式，以鳥瞰式透視，在大海中起平台，伸向天邊，海天相連，高朗空曠，境界深遠；另一種為封閉式，畫面中部起樓閣殿堂，堵滿空間，形成宮院內部庭園世界。這些都是中國首創的形式，具有獨特的民族特色。

綫與色是表現形式美的藝術語言，經過幾千年錘煉的綫，具有高度的概括力和表現功能，運筆中的輕重疾徐，抑揚頓挫，無不顯示鮮明的節奏和韵律感，通過律動感表現出形象的變化和生命力。

北朝秀勁瀟灑的鐵綫，創造了南朝士大夫典型的秀骨清像；隋唐豐潤而富於變化的藍葉描，則產生了宮娃般豐肥健美的菩薩。不同的綫，表現了不同的美。當然，不同的綫，也可以表現共同的美，綫本身沒有特殊個性。

色彩是敦煌藝術重要特色之一，它繼承了傳統繪畫色彩的象徵性、裝飾性和變色手法，創造了敦煌藝術的色彩美。早期壁畫的色彩鮮明而樸質，唐代則濃艷而輝煌，加上巧妙的變化和特殊手法，裝飾性的色彩美，登上了豪華富麗的頂峯。

無論外形式、內形式或表現形式的綫和色，都體現着對稱、均衡、賓主、疏密、主題突出、繁複而不紊亂、統一而不死板等形式美的規律，體現統一和諧之美。

人體美。中國繪畫自古主張"立象以盡意""寓形寄意"或者"以形寫神"，總之，重意不重象，重主觀不重客觀，重精神不重實體。漢晉以前，對人體美缺乏認識和理解，造型的真實感不佳，特別是裸體美，它與儒家倫理道德觀念水火不容。佛教傳入中國之後，熔印度、希臘、波斯藝術於一爐的佛教藝術，講究人體美的外來藝術，給敦煌藝術注入了新的血液，壁畫中的人體比例、面容姿態和立體感的表現大大提高，上身半裸的菩薩、天女、歌舞伎大量出現，翱翔太空的裸體飛天也偶露尊容。但是，中國繪畫反對"毛而失貌"，不贊成追求細節的真實而妨礙整體精神的表現，因而在造型中充分採取誇張變形手法，以塑造宗教理想的人物。王充說："譽人不增其美，則聞者不快其意，毀人不益其惡，則聽者不愜於心。"因而延伸人體比例，則人物瀟灑飄逸，如西魏的菩薩；人體比例縮短則強壯有力，如北魏的金剛力士；唐代菩薩身姿扭捏作"S"形，增強了"妍柔姣好"的女性美，如45窟盛唐的菩薩；楞眉鼓眼，挺腰揮拳，形如張弓，以示威武猛勇，如46窟的天王；至於天空神

怪，如獸頭人身的雷神、風神、三頭六臂的大自在天、象頭人身的比那夜迦等，則屬於想象組合的象徵形象。誇張則變形，即可創造出種種不曾有過的想象形象，以滿足宗教信仰和審美要求。

人體美的另一特色是立體感，敦煌早期壁畫接受了傳自龜茲的天竺明暗法，以朱紅重色，暗色暈染人體低凹處，烘托出凸起處，並在凸出部分塗以白色表示高明，使人體顯出圓渾的立體感，這就把美與真結合起來了。而中國壁畫則追求平面的裝飾美，以赭紅暈染人物面部兩頰，既表現紅潤色澤，也有一定的立體感。這兩種暈染法，一傳自西域，一來自中原，前者逼真感較強，後者象徵味更濃，各極其妙。

這兩種暈染法，經過長期融合至唐初合二為一，產生了一種既表現健美色澤，又富有立體感的暈染法。畫史上讚揚吳道子的人物畫，“形若脫壁”，“道子之畫如塑然”，“四面都可意會”，等等。這形成了敦煌壁畫的新風格。

戲劇性的美。敦煌壁畫有近百種故事，由於故事中曲折的情節和矛盾衝突，加上畫師們的匠心營構，賦予了這些故事畫、經變畫以戲劇性的美。最引人入勝的是悲劇性和喜劇性的題材。

有些壁畫屬於悲劇性，如早期的本生故事、因緣故事。佛教徒們在思想修煉中，要通過忍辱犧牲求得靈魂的完美才能成佛，因而犧牲者是樂意的，是沒有痛苦的。無論是捨身餵虎的薩埵王子，割肉貿鴿的尸毗大王，還是施頭千遍的月光王，以眼施人的快目王，他們的形象立刻恢復原貌，表情都是坦然自若安詳愉快的。雖然他們不能與革命者的從容就義相提

並論，但是他們的犧牲是為了“成佛”，為了求得超人的智慧和神力，“普濟眾生”這種捨己為人的犧牲精神，具有一定的悲劇性。特別是北魏254窟的《薩埵本生》，在藝術表現上取得了高度的成就。

壁畫中也有喜劇性的內容。《勞度叉鬥聖變》便是其中之一，描寫釋迦牟尼的弟子舍利弗與外道勞度叉鬥法的故事。佛經裡說，長者須達以黃金鋪地買祇陀太子園林為釋迦起精舍，外道要與佛徒鬥法，勝則建，敗則不能建。巨大的畫面，以舍利弗和勞度叉為主體，描寫六個鬥法場面：一、金剛智杵破邪山，二、威稜獅子噉水牛，三、六牙香象踏寶池，四、金翅鳥王鬥毒龍，五、毗沙門降黃頭鬼，六、旋嵐風掃盪六師。

畫師們把風樹之鬥作為最後決鬥場面，強勁的旋嵐風，吹開了舍利弗的勝利和勞度叉失敗的總體局面，勝利者舍利弗雍容大度，安詳自若，失敗者勞度叉驚惶失措，愁眉苦臉，寶座搖搖欲墜，徒眾們在慌亂中打椿、牽繩，加梯支撐。旋嵐風下，有的外道雙手遮面，暈頭轉向；有的以被遮掩，亂作一團；有的腦袋縮到胸部；有的羞怯地打恭受降；有的從胯下露出洗禮的光頭；有的剃髮後受到同伙的恥笑，雙手抱着光禿禿的腦袋發狂。整個畫面上莊嚴、鎮靜、安詳、欣慰與失敗、混亂、笨拙、可笑，形成強烈對比，在諷刺中體現了喜劇性的美。

最後談談風格美。風格是“誠於中而形於外”的多種審美因素的總體表現和最高表現。敦煌藝術的風格包括個人風格、畫派風格、地區風格、時代風格和民族風格。在封建社會裡，特別是邊遠地區，畫工塑匠地位低賤，加上師承傳授和宗教神靈形象陳陳相因的固定模

式，要自創風格頗不容易，因而個人風格、畫派風格，雖有而不明顯；最鮮明的是時代風格，由於政治、經濟、民族的變化，東西文化交流的影響，新的審美需要和審美理想的出現，促成了時代風格的不斷創新。十六國的西域風格，北魏的敦煌風格（或稱漢化的西域風格），西魏的南朝風格，隋唐的中原風格，五代、宋的瓜沙曹氏畫院風格，回鶻、西夏、元的密教風格，各具獨特風采，但同時也展現了貫穿各時代的民族精神和民族形式，這就是民族風格。

敦煌藝術民族風格有三大特點：

一、繼承了想象與現實相結合的創作方法，即以現實的形象，表現想象的神靈和虛幻的境界，合宗教想象和藝術想象於一體，而想象和幻想則是敦煌藝術創作的巨大動力。

二、我國傳統的形式美規律和表現技法，線、色、透視法、傳神技巧等，發揮了主導作用，把外來的宗教內容，特別是故事畫，從人物形象衣冠服飾和精神氣質，進行了多方面的中國化。

三、敦煌的藝術家們，大膽地不斷吸收融合外來藝術的新營養，促進了對人體美的觀念更新，使敦煌藝術從美與善的結合，進而美與真的結合，促進了真善美的三體合一。

上述三方面的結合，展現了敦煌藝術嶄新的民族風格和不朽的藝術生命，使之輝耀於世界文化藝術遺產之林。

THE RESPLENDENT ART OF DUNHUANG

by Duan Wenjie, president of Dunhuang Research Academy

I.

The art of Dunhuang comprises not only murals and painted sculpture, but architecture, paintings on silk, prints, calligraphy, music and dance, dyed fabrics, embroidery and other handicrafts. It is the entire complex of fine arts that were born and preserved at Dunhuang, in Gansu Province. Even more broadly, it includes as well Dunhuang's literature, the bianwen (prose and poetry derived from Buddhist sutras and other topics) and quci (songs, poetry and ballads) which are directly related to the murals.

Dunhuang's art is profoundly religious. All religions are born of history and develop along with human societies. And all religions are intimately intertwined with the fine arts. This has been true from the native religions of primitive man to the sophisticated religions that emerged after society had become stratified into classes. Religions use art to transmit their teachings and the arts, too, develop with religion.

Many treasures recorded in our history testify to this relationship of religion and art. For example: the ancient totems; the pre-historic pottery vessel depicting a fish with a human face; the late Zhou Dynasty painting on silk of a dragon fighting a phoenix, and a praying woman; the Warring States Period painting of an immortal ascending to heaven on the back of a dragon; the Western Han Dynasty painting on silk unearthed at Mawangdui in Hunan Province showing the spirits of the dead being guided to heaven; Gu Kaizhi's "Nymph of the Lo River;" and the Sixteen States Period tomb mural in Dingjiazha, Jiu Quan depicting the King of the East and the Queen of the West.

The same is true in the West. We can cite many universally acclaimed masterpieces with religious themes: the 20,000-year-old French cave mural at Lascaux showing wild bulls and bird-headed men; Greek statues and reliefs depicting the Olympian deities Zeus, Phoebus, the war god Ares and the goddess of wisdom Athena; and the murals in the Italian churches of the High Renaissance, such as Michelangelo's scenes from the creation on the ceiling of Sistine Chapel and Leonardo da Vinci's "The Last Supper."

The art of Dunhuang is Buddhist. The Magao and other adjacent grottoes in Dunhuang have a history that spans more than 1,000-years, from the Sixteen States period (303-402) to the Qing Dynasty (1644-1911). In the 570 known caves were discovered more than 50,000 square metres of murals, nearly 1,000 paintings on silk and hemp, 3,000 painted statues, 30,000 to 40,000 volumes of manuscripts and a number of dyed fabrics and embroidered works. These cultural relics, of extraordinary historical and artistic value, are the treasures of our country as well as the precious cultural heritage of mankind.

II.

The secular aspects of Dunhuang's art mirror everyday life of the past. Many different periods, nationalities, social classes and events were portrayed. People engaged in manual labour, singers and dancers, men and women experiencing the anguish of parting and happiness of reunion, social customs and local conditions, episodes from man's struggle with his fate, all contribute to the historical importance of Dunhuang's art.

MURALS

Many Chinese and foreign caravans traversing the ancient Silk Road were depicted in the murals. A most vivid scene is found in Cave 420. The caravan's owner is riding a horse, leading his silk-laden donkeys and camels on a journey to the west. A camel falls sick, and people examine it and treat it with an herbal potion. A donkey with a heavy load struggles painfully to climb a hill. Several people are pulling and pushing it. The caravan proceeds down the hill, and men grasp hold of the animals' tails.

Even so, one camel stumbles and the goods fall into a pool, splashing the water. A caravaner tumbles over a cliff, stands up, collects his goods, loads them onto another camel and continues on his way. Turning off into a valley, the caravan is robbed. After a fierce battle, all their merchandise is lost. These scenes faithfully portray the hazards of travel on the Silk Road in the Han to Tang dynasties. The old saying "Stop the merchants—Chinese and foreign—and levy taxes" carried great meaning in those days. During the Northern Zhou period, the governor of Liangzhou Prefecture intercepted and robbed foreign merchants. In the early Tang Dynasty, the monk Xuan Zhuang (Hsuan-tsang) encountered robbers in Central Asia. In the late Tang, Uyghurs stopped and robbed an envoy from Chinese emperor.

"The Emperor," part of a mural in Cave 220 dated AD 642, from the early Tang, is a masterpiece predating Yan Liben's "Portraits of Emperors of Previous Dynasties." Yan , a famous painter, was an official of high rank. The mural shows the Chinese emperor in splendid attire, wearing a broad robe. Two attendants hold feather fans to ward off wind and dust. They are followed by the emperor supported by ministers. One senior official is holding some manuscripts.

His hat is decorated with a marten tail signifying that the wearer enjoys a rank similar to that of prime minister. A group of kings and state leaders wearing felt or fur hats and in foreign dress with round collars and narrow sleeves, stand behind the ministers. They are showing their respects by cupping one hand in the other before their chests—a gesture not seen in the older paintings and portraits of emperors. According to historical records, after the Tang Emperor Taizong adopted a policy of "love all peoples as one," more than 100 leaders of various ethnic groups came to serve as officials in the Tang court at Chang'an. When the emperor made inspection tours, "kings and state leaders from neighbouring lands all followed." The same was true when Empress Wu Zetian went to confer a title on Mount Taishan. More than 10 Turkish, Persian, Khotanese and Kapisian leaders accompanied her.

In the narrative sutra mural in Cave 25 in Yulin, a wedding is underway. This was painted when Dunhuang was ruled by Tibetans. In a tent, long tables are heaped with fruits. The guests—men and women, Tibetans and Hans—sit side by side. The bridegroom and bride, accompanied by the best man and bridesmaid, are falling on their knees and performing obeisance. The groom, prostrating himself on the ground, is Tibetan. The bride, a silk shawl draped over her shoulders and a phoenix coronet on her head, is Han. The scene is both symbolic and reminiscent of the historic episodes of Princess Wencheng and Princess Jincheng marrying Tibetan rulers.

"Cultivation and Harvest" is a segment of a narrative sutra mural about Maitreya, the Buddha of the Future. It illustrates a wish in the sutra "Sow once and gather seven harvests." It begins with "Two Buffaloes in a Yoke." Th farmer is using a plough with a curved neck. The scenes that follow are harvesting, threshing, winnowing and storing the grain. The dou and hu measuring tools are nearby. A woman brings food and water to the field. The thirsty farmer, his head thrown back, is drinking his fill. In the hall, an official (or landlord) is sitting. A peasant is kneeling and delivering a report. Doesn't this vividly portray the collection of farm rents? It suggests that the farmers of the time farmed with great enthusiasm after the "equal land for all tillers" policy was implemented. It also shows that curved-neck ploughs had been introduced to Dunhuang from central China.

Many scenes of music and dance are found in the murals. They fall into two categories, divine and secular. The former refers to the heavenly musicians and dancers, or devas, in the paradise where the buddhas dwell; the latter to the music and dances of the mundane world.

The music and dance of the various ethnic peoples of the Hexi area (regions west of the Yellow River) were then collectively referred to as Western Liang music. Mostly this was the music of the Kutscha people and a blend of imported Hindu music and dance and those from central China. The "Dunhuang music" to which Wen Zisheng of the Northern Dynasty referred probably was a synthesis of these multiple elements.

The musical instruments in the mural include the zhen (plucked instrument), xiao and paixiao (bamboo flutes), fangxiang (a percussion instrument), sheng (reed pipe wind instrument), and ruanxian (a string instrument) from central China; the waist drum, qi drum, dala drum, jilou drum, five-stringed instrument, and bili (a wind instrument) from the Western Regions; and also instruments with foreign origins such as the pipa konghou (miniharp) and brass cymbal.

As for dance, there were some from the central plains of China and from the Western Regions. The former, with its melodious and refined music, featured the typical "elegant, long-sleeved dancers." In the Tang mural painting "Lady Song Guo Setting Forth on an Outing," there are four female dancers with their hair arranged in high knots. They wear long-sleeved blouses and skirts, and long silk scarves are draped over their shoulders. A Tang poem described dancers with "their graceful arms swaying, their long sleeves fluttering; then the sonorous songs, the notes sweetly reverberating."

The ethnic people of the Western Regions had a forward, direct manner, and spoke with great candour. They appeared quite emotional; the rhythm of their songs and dances was swift and even violent. A mural in Cave 220 shows two groups of people on small, round rugs. One is composed of male dancers wearing jewelled crowns and dhotis. Their arms are half bare and half covered by their silk costumes. The female dancers are half naked, wearing heavily pleated skirts, their long, loose hair fluttering.

Both groups swing around, tapping their toes on the floor in quick tempo, jumping high into the air. Overcome by the movement of dance and waving red scarves, they are like whirlwinds in the flickering light cast by wheel-shaped lamps. This is how Yuan Zhen described in his poem "a swaying foreign dancer"—"Black pearls glistening on her ears; colourful scarves rippling like rainbows, swift as lightning."

The history revealed in the art of Dunhuang is rich and colourful. It portrays the old international silk markets of the Han people sharing their communities with other peoples. It also documents the historical changes the area experienced in its cultural interminglings with countries to the west.

III.

Like all art, that of Dunhuang entrances by its beauty and its charm. And in the midst of aesthetic enjoyment, the viewer subliminally absorbs a religious message.

The art of Dunhuang is rich in variety.

Painted Statues.

Like all Buddhist sculptures, the painted statues of the deities are of human figures radiating wisdom and strength, as well as benevolence.

The giant statues of the Buddha convey a moral integrity and the complex spiritual dimensions of this supreme deity. The Northern Wei Period statue of the Dhyan Buddha expresses serenity and joy in meditation. Smiling faintly, his legs crossed and interlocked in Buddhist fashion, he appears detached from all worldly concerns. The Tang Dynasty statues of the mighty Heavenly Kings hold dagger-axes and swords, crushing devils under foot. Their gestures bespeak peace in heaven. The bodhisattvas of the Tang are invariably elegant and graceful, conveying a sense of mercy, compassion and helpfulness to those in distress. Their femininity has a characteristically Chinese beauty.

Paintings on Silk

About 700 to 800 paintings on silk, hemp cloth or paper were taken decades ago from what had been a sealed cave (now cave 17) in Dunhuang. Among these are narrative sutra pictures, portraits of Buddha and other deities and of donors, decorative patterns and picture-stories from Buddhist history. These had been stored in the cave for nearly 1,000 years and quite a few were heavily damaged. But most are still intact and vibrantly coloured. They are no longer in China and are as valuable as the grotto murals.

"Buddha Preaching Under a Bodhi Tree" is a masterpiece attributed to the early Tang. Sakyamuni sits under the tree with his legs interlocked in the posture of one preaching. He is dressed in a red samghati draped over one shoulder. Four bodhisattvas, of various demeanors, stand by the Buddha. Their black, flowing hair provides contrast to their rosy cheeks and bodies. Their thin, translucent silk scarves and capes enhance their ethereal appearance. The six disciples behind Buddha vary in demeanor, but all look amiable and light hearted. The woman donor kneeling by the pedestal wears a narrow-sleeved blouse and skirt. She clasps a lotus flower in both hands and conveys a sense of repose. Her hair is twisted into a knot, in a style similar to that of a woman donor in a mural in Cave 329. Both were painted by accomplished artists.

The self-contained composition "Buddha Preaching Under a Bodhi Tree" provides a vision of a mysterious and solemn realm where all is at peace and harmony.

The bodhisattva who serves as a guide to the souls of the dead in a painting on silk is a bearded man of almost feminine beauty. He walks over clouds, his left hand holding a lotus flower from which is suspended a vertical streamer—the gesture of the guide of souls. In his right hand is an incense burner, billowing fragrant clouds encasing the vision of a palace, the heavenly kingdom. The bodhisattva glances behind him, as if beckoning to the souls in his charge. The humble soul who trails behind him, a luxuriously dressed noble lady, resembles the women in the Tang Dynasty painter Zhou Fang's "Ladies Wearing Flowers." Her hair is specially arranged, in the paojiaji, and she wears a wide-sleeved jacket. Her hands are cupped together at her chest as she silently follows the bodhisattva. The theme—a guided journey to heaven—is wonderfully expressed in the composition. The woman and the misty clouds in the surrounding expanse are suspended in aesthetically harmonious balance.

Calligraphy

The tens of thousands of calligraphic works discovered in the sealed cave are in Chinese. They consist of works in various styles dating from the Eastern and Western Jin (265-420) to the Song (960-1279). These are rare works of art by amateurs. Many of the examples in the Scripture and the Regular scripts are exquisite.

The earlier Scripture Script was a transitional style developed from the lishu (clerical or official style) and the caoshu (grassy or running style) found incised on Han Dynasty bamboo slips. The kaishu (regular style) was developed after the Scripture Script. Most of the early Scripture Script works were done by such Dunhuang calligraphers as Suo Jing of the Jin Dynasty and Linghu Chongzhe and Cao Fashou of the Northern Wei.

The calligraphers working in this style must first draw fine lines, the wusilang to make columns of equal-size squares for the characters.

This guarantees the neatness of the finished work. The shape of the characters is similar to the clerical style, but the handling of the brush is different. When drawing horizontal lines, the writer must avoid pressing down too hard in order to ensure a thin line. But when the brush comes to the end of the line, it must be pressed down firmly. The solidity, roundness and fluency of the characters embody a quality that is both naive and beautiful. The calligraphic works attributed to Sui and Tang dynasties were mostly by menxiasheng and hongwenguan (official institutes) calligraphers in the capital of Changan. Hongwenguan scholar Ouyang Xun and monk Zhi Yong's works were popular in Dunhuang. They are neat, showing strong calligraphic strength and elegance, typical of Sui and Tang dyansty works.

Prints

Wood-block prints first appeared in Dunhuang in the early and High Tang periods. Most were monochrome, printed in black ink. Others were coloured by hand after printing.

The most famous prints include "Portrait of Avalokitesvara in the Posture of Lalitasana" of the High Tang period; an illustration of the Diamond Sutra dated 868: and the "Portrait of Vaisravana, "Printed at the expense of Cao Yuan Zhong.

The illustration of the Diamond Sutra "Buddha Preaching to Subhuti" is especially striking. In the centre Sakyamuni is seen from the side, preaching. His 10 disciples, Lokapalas the Heavenly King, and the heavenly guardian Vajrapanis are at left and right. Other disciples kneel by the pedestal.

The composition is very lively. The line is the sole artistic medium, but the engraving technique had reached such a high level that the thin, delicate lines are endowed with the strength, elegance and incisiveness of "thread-like iron wires." The contrast of the black and the white areas in the prints is good. The densely engraved areas and those with scant detail are well-balanced. The figures, though small, are vividly drawn.

Beauty in the Contents of Murals

As for the contents of the murals, some dismiss them as depicting merely deities and spirits, and as being weird and absurd. In fact, similarly critical comments were made in ancient times. But many of the narrative sutra murals are based on the Jataka stories written before Christ. Many are popular fables of ancient India and are beautifully written and quite wholesome.

A good example is the "Jataka of the Deer King." The Deer King, forgetting his own safety, jumped into a swift stream to rescue a drowning man. However, the man, blinded by greed, later betrayed his savior. When surrounded by troops of the king who controlled the region, the Deer King bravely condemned his ungrateful betrayer. The beauty of the story lies in the Deer King's moral integrity.

Another well-known Jataka story is "Xiang Hu and the Golden Elephant." When Xiang Hu was born, there appeared a golden elephant. They grew up together as constant companions. A peculiarity of the elephant was that his urine and feces turned into gold the moment they touched the ground. Hence, Xiang Hu's parents had gold all over their house. When Xiang Hu grew up, he went off to school. And one day, when his classmates were chatting about various strange things in their homes, Xiang Hu disclosed the secret of the elephant. Among his classmates was a prince. He made up his mind that once he became king, he would make the elephant his.

The prince later arranged to have his parents murdered and took the throne. Soon thereafter he asked Xiang Hu and his father to ride their elephant to a feast they were giving. The father and son were wonderfully treated, but this raised doubts in Xiang Hu's mind. "If this greedy king is so solicitous all of a sudden, there must be treachery a foot," he thought. Immediately he requested to leave. The king said his guests could go, but their elephant would have to stay. The father and son now realized what was going on, and walked out. The king caressed the elephant and was very pleased with himself. But suddenly the elephant sunk out of sight down into the earth, then reappeared outside the palace just in front of the father and son, who climbed atop the elephant rode home. The king got nothing for his plot or his feast. The charm of this fable lies in its humour.

Other murals, such as "Zhang Qian Setting Off to the Western Regions" and "Zhang Yichao Leading His Army on an Expedition," are about the heroic and patriotic deeds of historical figures.

All in all, the contents of the works of Dunhuang are rich and complex. Beauty as well as ugliness reside there. But for Chinese aestheticians, the beautiful and the ugly as well as their combination traditionally were predominant themes.

As for the question of beauty of artistic form, all spiritual or ideological messages must find fitting artistic vehicles for their expression. And it is by appreciating these artistic forms that the viewers' aesthetic feelings are aroused.

The artistic forms can be discussed at different levels.

External Form

First, the external form, as in the architectural structure of the Dunhuang grottoes.

In each cave there is a sunk panel or caisson ceiling in the shape of a canopy. This is always richly decorated, symbolizing heaven. The four walls bear painted portraits of the deities and narrative sutra stories to communicate the idea of paradise. In the primary niche are the statue of Buddha and his attendants, representing the supreme authority of the Buddhist world. The floor is paved with bricks displaying lotus patterns, representing the Buddhist Pure Land. The worshiper in a cave chapel felt he was in a Buddhist realm.

This is the external form, consisting of architecture, sculpture and murals. It is the expression of belief in a complex view of the true mission and meaning of life, a vision completely detached from the mundane world.

Every painting as well has an external form, appropriate to its contents. The single picture works well for one theme; a series of paintings is used express more than one theme. The multi-theme-continuous picture in the form of a horizontal or vertical scroll conveys a sense of changing times and seasons, different space and places, and complicated plots within one larger frame. The triptych placed the main picture and theme in the centre, flanked by two narrative sutra pictures, like couplets. All of these forms evolved to serve the needs of the contents.

Internal Form

By this we mean the various arrangements within paintings to communicate themes. For instance, the Natural Sequence Style refers to narrating a story in order from its beginning, through its development to its climax. The events of Buddha's life were treated this way, from the "Conception of Prince Siddhartha" to "Preaching in the Sarrath." The Conflict Style launches the narrative simultaneously from both the right and left ends of the painting and places the climax in the centre. "The Jataka of the Deer King" and the "Jataka of Samaka" are handled this way. The Climax Style begins immediately with the denouement, from whence the action subsides. The "Five Hundred Bandits Becoming Buddhas" illustrates this style.

The Moon-and-Satellites Style is for huge murals. The main theme is depicted in the centre, with subsidiary sutra stories forming a frame around it. This has two sub-styles. One is the Twin-Theme Style, in which two main figures face each other and the other illustrations are arranged between them. Examples of this are the illustration of the "Vimalakirtini Rdeśa Sutra" and the picture "Contest Between Sariputra and Raudraksa." The other, the Free Style, has the various narrative pictures randomly dispersed. There is no set pattern. In addition to illustrations of the sutras, most screen paintings are in this style.

Internal form determines the creation of a visionary space, or aesthetic vision. On the huge narrative sutra murals, there are two general types of composition. The Open-style composition is spacious and can provide, for example, a bird's eye view of a wide terrace extending far into the sea. The sea and the skies meet at a distant horizon creating an illusion of great depth. The Enclosed-style can be a scene of palace halls and pavilions, and so compactly constructed that little or no space is available for other objects. These usually are scenes of gardens inside the building compounds.

All the above are styles and compositional variations that have a unique national flavour.

Lines and Colours

Lines and colours are vehicles to create beauty. The use of lines has been developed for thousands of years in China. All objects, figures and scenes can be captured in highly expressive lines. A sense of rhythm and poetic charm are determined by how the brush is handled—pressed hard or lightly, in quick or slow motion, dabbed in staccato or held in suspense. The vitality and subtle nuances of the objects depicted are thus conveyed.

The thin but elegant and powerful "iron wire" lines used of the Northern Wei Dynasty shaped the typical "well-chiseled physiques and emaciated visages' of the literati of the Southern Dynasty (420-589). Through the use of varied and compact "orchid leaf" lines in Sui and Tang paintings, bodhisattvas were created on the model of the stout but elegant court ladies of the time. Thus, beauty is concentrated in its quintessential forms by the use of different lines. Of course, different lines can be used to capture this same beauty, for, there are no rigid rules governing the use of lines.

Colour is an important aspect of the art of Dunhuang. They are symbolic, decorative and variable in traditional Chinese painting. The earlier murals of Dunhuang are brightly coloured but simply applied while those of the Tang are richly and magnificently coloured. The latter also show skillful, intricate techniques in their application that help elevate the Tang murals to the highest level of decorative beauty.

All these external and internal forms, and the expressive use of lines and colours are wielded to create balance, symmetry, thematic prominence, intricacy without fussiness and unity without rigidity, and the rational combinations of primary and secondary elements, or of density and emptiness. All these are principles for creating beauty and for beauty to be embodied in harmony and unity.

Beauty in Human Figures.

Traditionally, Chinese artists and theoreticians held that "a portrait or image is meant to convey an idea," that "ideas are embodied in shapes," and that "the spirit is depicted through delineating the form." Generally, the stress is on ideas, not on shapes; on the subjective, not the objective; on the spirit, not on any substantial entity. People at that time saw little beauty in the human body. Hence, accurate, realistic representation was lacking in figure paintings. This was especially true regarding nudity. Even to discuss such things would have violated Confucian ethics.

When Buddhist art was introduced into China, it injected new blood into the art of Dunhuang. This exotic art form had already blended Greek, Indian and Persian elements and emphasized the beauty of human figures. This encouraged Chinese artists to give more accurate proportions to human figures, to capture realistic facial features and to endow figure painting in the murals with a three-dimensional quality. Occasional nude apsaras hover gracefully in the skies. Still, the notion that "too much of the particular blurs the picture" continued to influence Chinese artists. They believed that "over-adherence to details would cause the loss of the innate essence." This was why exaggeration was used in depicting ideal religious figures.

Wang Chong said: "If you don't over do it a bit when praising someone, the listeners won't feel so delighted. If you don't add more fault when condeming somebody, the audience won't be pleased." Hence, making human figures taller than life-sized was thought to add an elegant and refined air, as in the case of the bodhisattvas of the Western Wei period. When the human figure was deliberately drawn shorter, as was the Vajarapanis of the Northern Wei, the deity appeared robust and powerful. Tang bodhisattvas have S-shaped figures, such as the one of the High Tang period in Cave 45. The S-shape adds delicacy and grace to feminine beauty. The Lokapalas in Cave 46 have thick brows and round, protruding eyes. They stand firmly, waving their fists as if drawing an arrow against a bow. There is a group of symbolic heavenly beings such as the God of Thunder that has an animal's head on a human body, the God of Wind, the three-headed and six-armed Mahesvaras, and the elephant-headed and human-bodied Vinayaka. These were created out of man's imagination to meet people's aesthetic needs and to encode their religious faith.

Another aspect of the beauty of the human figure is its three-dimensional quality. Indian-style chiaroscuro was introduced to Dunhuang via Kutscha. Rich vermilion and other dark hues were coupled with white highlights to create a rounded, three-dimensional effect. All these done to blend the true with the beautiful. Conventionally, Chinese mural artists had sought beauty through the decorative quality of flat colours. They applied rose-red to the cheeks, to give a slightly three-dimensional quality. The method of applying colours and washes from the Western Regions was more representational. The Chinese method was more symbolic. Each had its advantages.

The two approaches merged during the Tang Dynasty, resulting in a new one that blended these advantages. Chinese art historians praised the figure paintings of Wu Daozi: "Daozi's figures are like sculpture." "One can admire them from four sides." This became a new style in Dunhuang's murals.

Dramatic Beauty

There are nearly a hundred sutra and other stories depicted in the murals. The intrigues of plots and conflicts, and the artists' creative efforts rendered them into dramatically beautiful works of art. Most notable are the tragic and comic subjects.

The tragic ones include the early Jataka and Hetupratyaya stories. Buddhists, when undergoing spiritual tempering, must endure humiliation and self-sacrifice to purify and perfect their souls. Hence, those who sacrificed their lives did so voluntarily and did not suffer. This is why they are portrayed as fully recovered from every kind of brutality. Examples include Prince Mahasattva, who fed a hungry tiger with his own body; King Sivi, who sliced off his own flesh to feed a dove; the Moonlight King, who gave up his own head thousands of times; and King Sudhira, who gave his eyes to a demon. They all appear calm and happy in the murals, for they have sacrificed themselves to achieve Buddhahood, the highest wisdom and divine grace. They existed for "the salvation of all human lives on earth." There was indeed a tragic element in their self-sacrifice. The "Prince Mahasattva Jataka" in Cave 254 of the Northern Wei period is of especially high artistic quality.

There are also comic episodes, such as the "Contest Between Sariputra and Raudraksa," recounting how Sariputra, a disciple of Sakyamuni, won over a pagan. According to the sutra, Drhapati Sudatta spread gold over the grounds of Prince Jata's garden. He wanted to buy the land to build a fine residence for Sakyamuni. The pagan Raudraksa suggested a contest. If he won, then nobody would build the residence. The huge mural takes the two contesting parties as the main foci, and displays six scenes of contest: 1. The Vajra Taking the Wicked Mountain; 2. The Lion Devouring the Buffalo; 3. The Six-Tusked Elephant Tramping About the Treasure Pond; 4. The Golden-Winged King Garuda Fighting the Venomous Dragon Naga; 5. Vaisravana Conquering the Yellow Headed Devil; 6.The Whirlwind Sweeping Away the Demons.

The mural artists made the last item the final battle to show how Sariputra won his victory in the whirlwind and Raudraksa was defeated.

The victor appears dignified, graceful and poised; the vanquished frightened and distressed. The latter's pedestal is shaky. His followers are in a flurry driving piles, pulling ropes and setting up ladders to prop it up. In the whirlwind, some of the pagans are covering their faces with their hands; others are taking refuge under quilts; still others drop their heads to their chests. One pagan is sheepishly folding his hands in surrender. Another's bald head is seen under his hip after the ceremony to initiate him into monkhood. Some, after being shaved, hold their bald heads in a frenzy as they suffer the ridicule of

their companions. The picture sets up strong contrasts between dignity and composure on one hand and confusion, failure, stupidity and ludicrousness on the other. But in this humour there is dramatic beauty.

Beauty in Style

Style is the highest expression of the relevant aesthetic elements that is "innate but still can be seen." The different styles at Dunhuang include those of individual or groups of artists, local styles, styles of various periods and of various nationalities.

In ancient, feudal China, especially in remote areas such as Dunhuang, artisans or folk artists crafted the murals and statues but were ranked among the lowest levels of society. The rigid system of apprenticeship to a mast to learn the trade, and the demand that only certain established ways of fashioning religious portraits, be followed made it very difficult for artists to develop individual styles. Therefore, although we could talk about their styles, they are not very distinctive. The greatest differences in style stem from successive historical periods. This came about through political, economic and ethnic influences and cultural exchanges between East and West and also due to new aesthetic needs and ideals that would occasionally emerge. All these led to constant evolutions in style imprinted with the characteristics of various periods.

Those that are distinctive and unique include the Western Regions style of the Sixteen States period, the Dunhuang style (or Sinicized Western Regions style) of the Northern Wei period, the Southern Dynasty style of the Western Wei period, the Central Plains style of the Sui and

Tang dynasties, the Cao Family Painting Academy style of the Guasha area in the Song Dynasty and the Esoteric Buddhism Style of the Uyghur, Western Xia and Yuan dynasties. In these styles of various periods are integrated the spirit and artistic forms of various ethnic peoples and their national styles.

Dunhuang can be listed that illustrate the national Chinese style:

1. Methodologically, the art of Dunhuang carried on the tradition of combining imagination and realism. Realistic forms from life were manipulated to illustrate visionary deities, spirits and illusory realms. Religious and artistic imagination were integrated into one, and imagination and illusion provided powerfully driving forces for artistic creation.

2. Traditionally, Chinese techniques and principles for creating beauty, as in the use of lines, colours, the peculiarly Chinese form of multiple perspectives, and rules for portraiture dominated Dunhuang. The exotic religious contents and certainly the human figures, their costumes and coiffures, their manners and postures, depicted in sutra and other stories were sinicized by various methods.

3. The folk artists of Dunhuang boldly assimilated elements from foreign sources. This helped to transform their concept of the beauty of the human figure and enabled the art of Dunhuang to move from a combination of the beautiful and the good, to a combination of the beautiful and the genuine. Ultimately, there was a synthesis of the genuine, the good and the beautiful.

A new national style and spirit thus emerged from this synthesis and it has earned the art of Dunhuang a rightful place in the cultural heritage of the world.

輝かしい敦煌芸術

段文傑

（ 一 ）

敦煌芸術は敦煌から生み出され、そこにたくわえられている多分類の芸術総合体であり、敦煌壁画と敦煌彩塑を指しているばかりでなく、この中には敦煌建築、敦煌絹絵、敦煌版画、敦煌書道、敦煌舞楽や敦煌染織やししゅうなどの工芸美術が含まれている。一般的には敦煌文学、変文、曲辞など壁画と直接関係のあるものも含まれるべきだ。

敦煌芸術は宗教芸術であり、仏教題材の芸術である。莫高窟を中心とする敦煌石窟は、十六国から元、清までの千余年を経過し、現存洞窟570箇以上、壁画五万平方メートル余り、帛画およそ千幅、彩塑およそ三千体、写本三、四万点と一組の染織ししゅうがある。わが国の民族芸術の宝として、すべてが高い歴史的価値と芸術的価値を持ち、世界でもまれな宝であり、わが国の民族的芸術珍宝と人類の文化遺産の玉としてその名に恥じない。

（ 二 ）

現実の生活を反映している面から言えば、敦煌芸術は世俗芸術と同様に歴史の鏡である。壁画と絹絵の中から異った時代や民族と階層のさまざまな物事例えば労働生産や太平な世の中や、悲しみと喜びや風土と人情および人類の歴史的運命などがうかがわれる。

敦煌壁画にはシルクロードを奔走する中国と西方の隊商がかなり描かれてあり、その中の第420窟に見られる隊商は特にいきいきしている。この絵は漢唐以来のシルクロードの危難を真実に反映している。

初唐の第220窟の貞観十六年の「帝王出行図」は当時大臣をつとめていた著名な画家閻立本の傑作「歴代帝王図」より年代が前だ。

楡林窟吐蕃時代第25窟の「弥勒変」の中の嫁娶図は画青廬（とばり）の中で結婚式をあげている場面である。とばりの中に長机が設けられ、くだもの類が置かれ、男女賓客や蕃漢族が共に席につき、びょうぶの中の花嫁と花婿はそれぞれの付添人に仕えられながらひざまずいて拝礼している。五体を地にうつぶしている花婿は吐蕃族で、鳳冠をかむり絹織物をまとっている花嫁は漢族である。この漢蕃族連姻図は、文成姫がチベットへ嫁ぎ、金城姫が蕃族と結婚したことをシンボルにして描いたものである。

盛唐期第454窟の「弥勒変」の中の耕獲図は仏経「一種七収」の一語によって描かれ、「二牛抬槓」から始まり、農夫の土地の耕し、種まき、刈り取り、脱穀や風選、穀物の山積み、地面に散らばっているますなどの量器が描かれ、農婦は畑のはしから水と食糧を持って来て、飢えてのどが渇いている農夫達は水の入ったつぼを抱え痛飲している。広間には赤いころもをまとった官吏（あるいは地主）がすわり、農夫はひざまずいて上申している。

敦煌壁画の中にはかなりの数の舞楽の場面があるが、主なものは天楽と俗楽である。天楽とは仏国世界の舞楽をさし、俗楽とは世の中の生活画面中の舞楽で、主に河西にはやっていた西涼楽を指している。西涼楽とは西域各民族の舞楽で、主に亀茲楽と天竺楽を加えたもので、中原舞楽と結びつけた舞楽である。舞踏からみるとその中には長い袖を振り

まわしておだやかにひらひらと舞いおどる中原舞があり、いわゆる「長袖善舞」は正に中原舞の特長である。このほか西域民族の率直な性格や激しい感情を表わす強いリズムの西域舞がある。

とにかく敦煌芸術には豊富多彩な歴史がたくわえられていて、それは漢族を主体とする多民族が集まり住んでいた国際シルク市場と中西文化交流の国際都会の変遷史の鏡である。

（ 三 ）

敦煌芸術はその他の芸術と同様に美を作り出し、多くのすぐれた作品はその強烈な芸術魅力で人々を引きつけ、人々が楽しむ中で宗教宣伝を発揮する作用を持っている。

敦煌芸術美も多種多様である。

敦煌彩塑はすべての仏教彫塑と同じく真実の人間像を借りて神霊の知恵と力を象徴し、善良で素晴らしい望みを象徴している。

敦煌絹絵は蔵経洞の中から見つけられた絹本と紙本画を指し、目下知られているのが七、八百幅余りに達し、内容は非常に豊富である。その中には各種類の経変、仏ぼさつ像、仏教史跡画、供養人画像や装飾図案などがある。倉庫の中に千年近く置かれていたため、ひどく痛められているが、多くの画像ははっきりしていて色彩も格別にあざやかで美しい。これらの略奪された宝物は石窟壁画と同様に貴重である。

敦煌書道は蔵経洞で発見された数万件の漢文写本を指し、この中には両晋南北朝から宗代までの各種の書道が含まれている。これら

は大量の民間書道芸術珍品で、その中の写経体と楷書にはすぐれたものが非常に多い。

敦煌版画は盛唐の初期からすでにあらわれ、木版単線彫刻、墨色刷印、そして刷印後着色するものもある。例えば盛唐初期の遊戯座観音菩薩、晩唐咸通九年（868年）の「金剛経」のさしえ「祇樹給孤獨園図」それから五代開運四年（947年）曹元忠施北方毗沙門天王像など。特に「祇樹給孤獨園図」は釈迦牟尼仏が側面から説教していて、十大弟子、釈梵天王、金剛力士が両側を取り囲み、台座の下には仏の弟子がひざまずいている。この図は構成が活発で、彫刻の技術も精ちである。線は造型の唯一の芸術的言語で、線刻技術はすでに高度に熟練し、全体は力強く、白黒は互いに引き立てられ、疎密の度合いはよく、人物は小さいが生き生きとして線の力感美が充分にあらわれている。

美しい内容。ある人達は敦煌壁画の内容の中には神や亡霊が語られ、奇妙で荒誕だと言っており、古人も昔から批判しているが、物語の多くは紀元前の書物「本生経」からのもので、多くはインドの民間ぐう言物語であるから内容は健康で美しいのである。

敦煌芸術の内容は豊富で複雑で、その中には美しいものもあるし、みにくいものもあるが、美と善は中国美学思想の美と善を結合したものを体現し、これが中心である。

美しい形式。敦煌芸術の形式は多種類の段階がある。例えば外形式はそれぞれの洞窟の組み立てが立体的で、上には空を象徴する天井を設け、周壁画の神霊像は巨型な経変をなして極楽の幻境を示し、正龕に仏陀と脇侍を設け、仏国世界の支配者を象徴している。地面にははすの模様のあるれんがをしき、浄土を象徴し、人々が洞の中へ入ると仏国に来たような感じがする。

それぞれの絵にもその内容に適応する外部の形式がある。一幅の絵は単一のテーマを表わす形式で、一組の絵は多種類のテーマを表わす連合形式である。連続式は異なった時間、空間と曲折な筋を表わす横巻式あるいは立軸式、三連式つまり三位一体式は主題画の両側にたいれん式故事画を配置するように、これらの形式はすべて内容にしたがう民族絵画形式の新しい発展である。

内形式とは画面上の主題思想の内容を表わす構成で、これにもさまざまなものがある。例えば物語の発生、発展、クライマックスと終りの法則にしたがって陳列する順序式がある。又始りと終りの両側から始り、画面の中部で矛盾が衝突し、クライマックスに達しそれで物語が終る衝突式がある。例えば「九色鹿本生」や「睒子本生」など。それから始めから衝突のクライマックスが展開され、そのあと調子がしだいに下げられていくクライマックス式がある。例えば「五百強盗成仏」がこれである。多くの星が月を取りまいていると言う意味の衆星拱月式は色々な物語を主体画面のまわりに配置し、求心型構造をなす巨型経変はこの種類に属するものが多い。双主体式は二名の主体人物が遠くから向かい合い変化自在の通力を示す。「維摩変」や「労度叉闘聖変」はみなこの種類に属する。自由式は物語の筋を随意にアレンジし進ませたり、戻らせたりあるいは左右に織り込ませたり方則がなく、経変に織り込まれた物語やびようぶに描かれた絵の多くがこの種類に属する。

内形式に対する要求は空間境界を創造することで、多くが巨型経変の中に体現され、大体二種類の構図に分けられる。ひと種類は開方式で、バーズ・アイ式に透視し、大海中に平台を築き、天辺まで伸ばし、海天相連で、境界深遠である。もうひと種類は密封式で、画面中部に楼閣殿堂を築き上げ、空間をうずめ、宮庭内部の庭園世界をなす。これらはすべて中国が初めて作り出した形式で、独特の民族特色をそなえている。

線と色は形式美を表現する芸術的言語で、幾千年を経てみがきあげられた線は高度な概括力と表現効能をそなえ、運筆中の軽重疾徐、抑揚や休止の工合はみな鮮明なリズムと韻律感を示し、形象的変化と生命力を表わしている。

色彩は敦煌芸術の重要な特色のひとつであり、伝統的絵画の色彩のシンボル性、装飾性と変色手方を受け継いで、敦煌芸術の色彩美を作り出している。早期壁画の色彩は鮮明で質樸で、唐代のは濃えんで輝かしい、それに巧妙な変化と特殊な手法を加えてあるので、装飾性の色彩美は豪華で華麗の最高峰に達している。

外形式も内形式も形式を現わす線も色もすべてが対称、均衡、主客、疎密、主題のきわ立ち、繁複しかもびん乱でない、統一しかも生き生きしているなどの形式美の法則を体現し、統一で調和がとれている美しさを体現している。

人体美。中国絵画は昔から意を重視し、像を重視しなく、主観を重視し、客観を重視しなく、精神を重視し、実体を重視しないことを主張している。漢晋以前は人体美に認識と

理解が欠けていて、造形の真実感がよくなかった。特に裸体美は儒家の論理道徳観念と氷炭相容れなかった。仏教が中国に伝われてからインドやギリシアやペルシアの芸術をひとつのかまどで溶かした仏教芸術や人体美を重んずる外来芸術は敦煌芸術に新しい血液を注入し、壁画中の人体比例や容ぼうや姿や立体感の表現力は大いに上達し、上身が半裸の菩薩や天女や歌舞伎が数多く現われ、高空を飛びまわる裸体飛天もたまにはその姿を見せるようになった。しかし、中国絵画は細かい真実を追求し、精神総体の表現をさまたげることに不賛成で、造形中誇張で、変形した手法を充分用いて理想的な宗教人物を作りあげていた。

人体美のもうひとつの特色は立体感で早期の敦煌壁画は亀茲から伝わって来た天竺明暗方を引き受け朱色をさかんに使い、濃い色で人体のくぼんでいる所を染め、突き出ている所をきわだたせている。そして突き出ている所を白色で塗り、立派に見せ、人体をまるみのある立体感に見せて、美と真を結び付けている。しかし中国壁画は平面の装飾美を追求して赤かっ色で人物の両ほほを染め、赤くつややかに見せているので一定の立体感がある。この二種類の彩色のほどこし方の中ひとつは西域から、もうひとつは中原から伝わったもので、前者は真に迫って、後者はシンボル的である。

このふたつの採色のほどこし方は、長期間の融合の結果唐の初期に合併し、健美のいろつやを表現すると同時に立体感を富むものになって、敦煌壁画の新風格を成した。

ドラマチツク美。敦煌壁画には百点に近い物語があり、物語の筋が曲折で矛盾衝突の上画家たちが工夫して作りあげたため、これらの故事画や経変画はドラマチックな美を示している。一番人を引きつけているのは悲劇的と喜劇的題材の物語である。

ある壁画は悲劇的題材に属する。例えば早期の本生故事や因縁ばなしである。教徒が思想修練中聖者になるため、恥をしのび身を犠牲にし霊魂を清めなければならない。したがって犠牲者は苦痛を覚えず喜んで身を犠牲にしていた。捨身飼虎のサッタや割肉貿鴿のシビなど彼達の姿はただちに元にもどり、表情もみな泰然自若で落ちつき、愉快になっている。聖者になるため、超人的な知恵と力を求めるため、このような人のために身を犠牲にする精神は、一定の悲劇性を備えている。特に北魏の第254窟の「サッタ本生」は、芸術表現上大きな成果を収めている。

最後にスタイル美について述べてみる。スタイルとは多種審美要素の総体表現と最高表現である。敦煌芸術のスタイルには個人スタイルや画流スタイルや地域スタイルや時代スタイルや民族スタイルが含まれる。封建社会では特に辺境の地では画工や彫刻師の地位が低くかった上、師匠からの伝授と宗教神霊像が陳腐で全然新味がない固定化したパターンであったため、みずから新たなスタイルを作り出すのはきわめて難かしかった。したがって個人スタイルや画流スタイルはあったが、区別はあまりなかった。もっとも鮮明なのは時代スタイルで、政治や経済や民族に変化があったため、そして東西文化交流の影響や新しい審美の必要と審美理想の出現から新しい時代スタイルが次から次へと生み出された。

十六国の西域スタイルや北魏の敦煌スタイルや西魏の南朝スタイルや隋唐の中原スタイルや五代、宋の瓜沙曹氏画院スタイルや回鶻、西夏、元の密教スタイルなどはそれぞれユニークな風さいを持っているが、同時に各時代をつらぬく民族精神と民族形式が展開されている。これが民族スタイルである。

敦煌芸術の民族スタイルには三大特色がある。

一、想像と現実を結び付けた創作方法を継承している。すなわち現実的像をもって想像中の神霊と夢幻の境界をあらわし、宗教的想像と芸術的想像を一体にし、しかも想像と幻想は敦煌芸術の創作の巨大な原動力である。

二、わが国の伝統的形式美の法則と表現技法や線、色、透視法や生き生きとして真に迫る技法は主導の役割を果し、外来の宗教内容特に絵物語の中の人物像の衣冠服飾や精神気質など各方面に対しては中国風であるようにしている。

三、敦煌の芸術家達は、外来芸術の新しい栄養を大胆に、たえまなく吸収して融合し、人体美に対する観念の更新を促がし、敦煌芸術を美と善の結合からひいては美と真の結合にし、真善美の三体合一を促進した。

以上の三点の結合は、敦煌芸術の真新しい民族スタイルと不朽な芸術生命を展開し、世界文化芸術の遺産の中でその光をかがやかせている。

（本訳文には若干の省略がある。）

北涼
Northern Liang
北涼

輝煌的壁畫
·
Resplendent
Mural Paintings
·
輝かしい壁画

1. 斗四藻井天宮伎樂
   第272窟
   Square Ceiling and
   Heavenly Musicians
   cave 272
   斗四藻井天宮伎楽
   272窟

2. 供養菩薩　　第272窟龕南

Attendant Bodhisattvas
cave 272

供養菩薩　　272窟龕南

3. 供養菩薩　　第272窟龕北
Attendant Bodhisattvas
cave 272
供養菩薩　　272窟龕北

17

4. 遊觀見老苦　　第275窟南壁
The Encounter with Old Age　　cave 275
遊観見老苦　　275窟南壁

5. **毗楞竭梨王身釘千釘**
第275窟北壁

Jātaka of King Bi-leng-jie-li
cave 275

ビリンジェリ王本生
275窟北壁

6. 三佛説法圖　　第263窟南壁
A Triad of Buddhas Preaching the Law　　cave 263
三仏説法図　　263窟南壁

8. 夜半逾城　　第431窟　中心柱南向龕西側
Siddhārtha Crosses over the Wall　　cave 431
夜半逾城　　431窟　中心柱南向龕西側

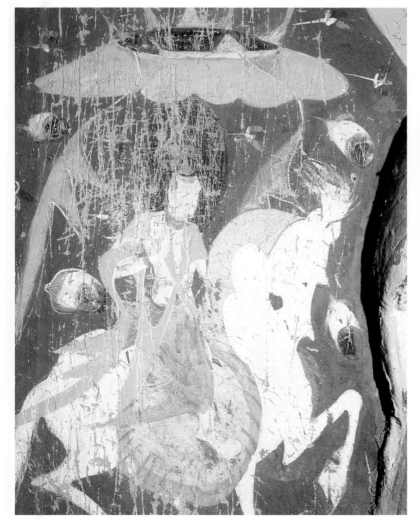

7. 乘象入胎　　第431窟　中心柱南向龕東側
Conception of Prince Siddhārtha　　cave 431
乘象入胎　　431窟　中心柱南向龕東側

11. **九色鹿救溺人**　　第257窟西壁

Jataka of the Deer King (section)　　cave 257

　　九色鹿救溺人　　257窟西壁

9. **天宮伎樂**
　　第248窟北壁

Musicians in a Heavenly
Palace　　cave 248

　　天宮伎楽　　248窟北壁

10. 金剛力士　　第254窟西壁
Vajrapani　　cave 254
金剛力士　　254窟西壁

12. 沙彌守戒自殺之一
    第257窟南壁

    Hetupratyaya of the Śrāmanera Commiting
    Suicide for Observing the Sila (1)
    cave 257

    沙弥守戒自殺部分（1）
    257窟南壁

13. 沙彌守戒自殺之二
    第257窟南壁

    Hetupratyaya of the Śrāmanera Commiting
    Suicide for Observing the Sila (2)
    cave 257

    沙弥守戒自殺部分（2）
    257窟南壁

14. 沙彌守戒自殺之三
第257窟南壁

Hetupratyaya of the Śrāmaṇera Commiting
Suicide for Observing the Sīla (3)
cave 257

沙弥守戒自殺部分（3）
257窟南壁

15. 沙彌守戒自殺之四
第257窟南壁

Hetupratyaya of the Śrāmaṇera Commiting
Suicide for Observing the Sīla (4)
cave 257

沙弥守戒自殺部分（4）
257窟南壁

16. 薩埵捨身飼虎
第254窟南壁

Jātaka of Prince Sudana
cave 254

サツタ捨身飼虎
254窟南壁

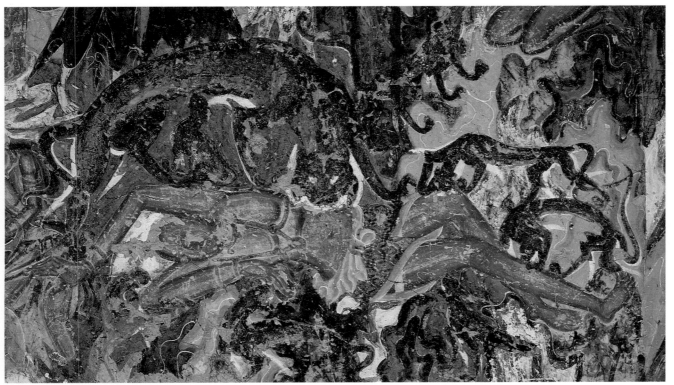

17. 薩埵捨身飼虎（局部）
第254窟南壁

Jātaka of Prince Sudana
(section)
cave 254

サツタ捨身飼虎
（局部）
254窟南壁

18. 尸毗王割肉貿鴿　　第254窟北壁
Jātaka of King Šivi　　cave 254
シビ王割肉貿鴿　　254窟北壁

19. 窟室（局部） 　　第288窟主室
 Shape of the cave (section)　　cave 288
 窟室（局部）　　288窟主室

20. 藻井・諸天神　　第249窟
Square Ceiling and Deities　　cave 249
天井・諸天神　　249窟

21. 東王公　　第249窟北披
East-King-father
cave 249
東王公　　249窟北披

22. 西王母　　第249窟南披　　West-queen-mother　　cave 249　　西王母　　249窟天井南面
23. 伏羲女媧　　第285窟東披　　Fuxi and Nuwa　　cave 285　　伏羲女媧　　285窟天井東面

24. 說法圖　　第288窟北壁
Buddha Preaching the Law　　cave 288
説法図　　288窟北壁

25. 供養菩薩　　第249窟北側
Attendant Bodhisattva　　cave 249
供養菩薩　　249窟北側

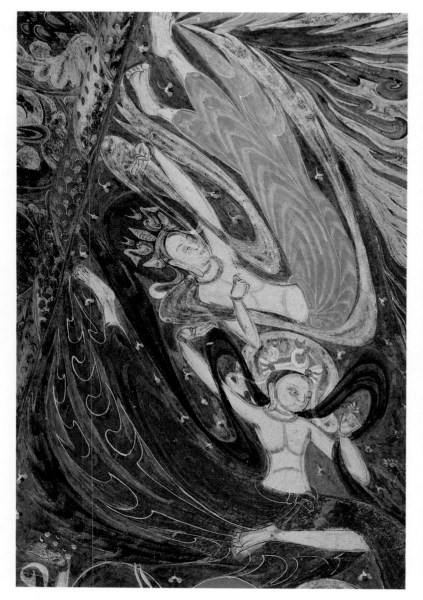

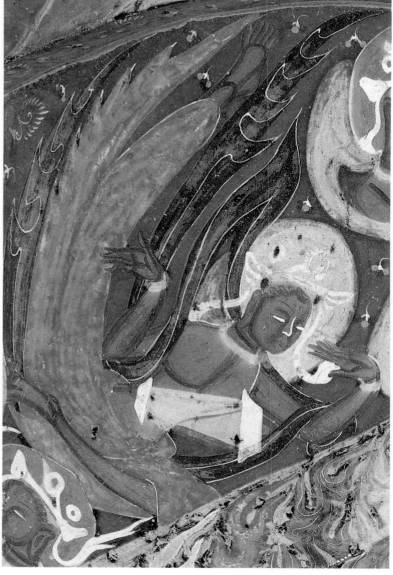

26. 飛天　　　第285窟龕頂
Apsaras　　　cave 285
飛天　　　285窟龕頂

27. 飛天　　　第249窟龕頂
Apsaras　　　cave 249
飛天　　　249窟龕頂

28. 化生童子　　第285窟正龕楣
Reborn Children　　cave 285
化生竜子　　285窟正龕楣

29. 天宮伎樂　　第249窟南壁
Musicians in a Heavenly Palace　　cave 249
天宮伎楽　　249窟南壁

30. 天宮伎樂　　第288窟西壁
Musicians in a Heavenly Palace　　cave 288
天宮伎楽　　288窟西壁

31. 天宮伎樂　　第288窟西壁
    Musicians in a Heavenly Palace　　cave 288
    天宮伎楽　　288窟西壁

32. 金剛力士　　第249窟北壁
    Vajrapanis　　cave 249
    金剛力士　　249窟北壁

33. 金剛力士　　第288窟中心柱南側
　　Vajrapanis　　cave 288
　　金剛力士　　288窟中心柱南側

34.　護法諸天　　第285窟西壁正龕北側　　Devas　　cave 285
　　　護法諸天　　285窟西壁正龕北側

35.　護法諸天　　第285窟西壁正龕南側　　Devas　　cave 285
　　　護法諸天　　285窟西壁正龕南側

36. **天界諸神**　第285窟西披
     Deities　cave 285
     天界諸神　285窟天井西面

37. **狩獵圖**　第249窟北披
     Scene of Hunting　cave 249
     狩猟図　249窟天井北面

38. 禪廬・黃羊・老虎
第285窟東披
Scene of Dhyana
cave 285
禅廬・黃羊・虎
285窟天井東面

39. 禪廬・宰野豬・獵野羊
第285窟南披
Scene of Dhyana   cave 285
禅廬・いのしし殺し・黃羊狩リ
285窟天井南面

40. **作戰圖**　　第285窟南壁
Battle　　cave 285
戦ろ図　　285窟南壁

北周
Northern Zhou
北周

41. **降魔變**　　第428窟北壁
　　Vanquishing Māra　　cave 428
　　降魔変　　428窟北壁

43. **擲象・相撲**　　第290窟人字披
　　Throwing Elephant and Wrestling
　　cave 290
　　象投げ・スモウ　　290窟人字披

44. **射鐵鼓**　　第290窟人字披
　　Shooting Iron-drums　　cave 290
　　鉄鼓射　　290窟人字披

42. **福田經變**　　第296窟北披
Illustration of Fu Tian Sutra　　cave 296
福田経変　　296窟天井北面

45. 藻井・裸體飛天　　第428窟西披
Naked Apsaras in the Square-
ceiling　　cave 428

天井・裸體飛天　　428窟西披

46. 飛天・菩薩　　第428窟南壁
   Apsaras and Bodhisattvas　　cave 428
   飛天・菩薩　　428窟南壁

47. 胡人馴馬　　第290窟中心柱西側
   Foreigner Training Steed　　cave 290
   胡人馴馬　　290窟中心柱西側

43

隋代
Sui Dynasty
隋代

48. 中心塔柱　第303窟
Central Stupa-pillar
cave 303
中心塔柱　303窟

49. 三兔蓮花藻井　　第407窟
Lotus-square-ceiling with Three
Rabbits　　cave 407
三兔蓮花天井　　407窟

50. 須達拏本生　　第419窟東披
Jātaka of Sudana　　cave 419
スダーナ本生　　419窟天井東面

46

51. 菩薩　第420窟西壁北側
Bodhisattvas　cave 420
菩薩　第420窟西壁北側

47

52. 執拂天女　　第62窟西壁
Attendant Goddess　　cave 62
はたきを持つ天女　　62窟西壁

53. 供養馬車・山林人物
第303窟東壁
Cart, Horse, Forest
and Figures
cave 303
供養車馬と山林人物
303窟東壁

初唐
Early Tang
初唐

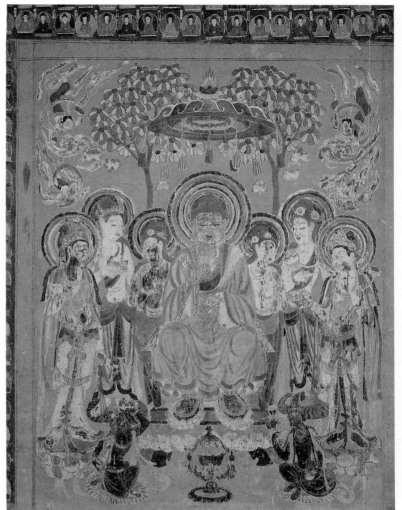

54. 説法圖　　第322窟南壁
Buddha Preaching the Law　　cave 322
説法図　　322窟南壁

55. 菩薩・弟子　　第57窟南壁
Bodhisattvas and Disciple　　cave 57
菩薩・弟子　　57窟南壁

56. **文殊・聽法帝王**　　第220窟東壁
Manjusri and Emperor　　cave 220
文殊・帝王聽法　　220窟東壁

57. **思維菩薩**　　第71窟北壁
Meditating Bodhisattva　　cave 71
思維菩薩　　71窟北壁

58. 菩薩
第334窟龕頂北側
Bodhisattva
cave 334

菩薩
334窟龕頂北側

59. 舞樂之一　　第220窟北壁東側
Orchestra (section 1)　　cave 220
舞楽その一　　220窟北壁東側

60. **舞樂之二**　　第220窟北壁西側
　　Orchestra (section 2)　　cave 220
　　舞楽その二　　220窟北壁西側

61. 藻井・飛天　　第329窟
Apsaras in Square-ceiling　　cave 329
天井・飛天　　329窟

62. **各國王子**
第220窟東壁
Princes of Various Countries
cave 220

各国王子 220窟東壁

63. **群臣** 第220窟東壁
Ministers cave 220
衆臣 220窟東壁

64. 各族君長　　第220窟東壁
　　Heads of Vairous Nationalities　　cave 220
　　各族郡長　　220窟東壁

65. 馬夫・馬　　第431窟南壁
　　Groom and Steed　　cave 431
　　馬丁と馬　　431窟南壁

盛唐
High Tang
盛唐

66. 化城喻品　　第217窟南壁
Parable of the Illusory City　　cave 217
化城喻品　　217窟南壁

67. **胡商遇盗**　　第45窟南壁
Merchants Encountering with Robbers
cave 45

胡商遇盗　　45窟南壁

68. 菩薩　　第217窟北壁
Bodhisattvas　　cave 217
菩薩　　217窟北壁

70. 弟子頭像　　第217窟龕內北側
Head of Disciple　　cave 217
弟子頭像　　217窟龕內北側

69. 菩薩頭像　　第45窟龕內南側
Head of Bodhisattva　　cave 45
菩薩頭像　　45窟龕內南側

71. 飛天穿梭
第217窟北壁

Apsaras　　cave 217

飛天楼閣通し
217窟北壁

72. 男剃度圖
第445窟北壁

Tonsure of the Men
cave 445

男剃髪図
445窟北壁

73. **女剃度圖**　　第445窟北壁
Tonsure of the Women　　cave 445
女剃髪図　　445窟北壁

74. 舞樂圖之一　　第154窟北壁
Orchestra (section 1)　　cave 154
舞楽図部分（1）154窟北壁

75. **舞樂圖之二**　　第154窟北壁
Orchestra (section 2)　　cave 154
舞楽図部分（2）154窟北壁

76. 反彈琵琶伎樂
第112窟南壁

Dancer
cave 112

反弾琵琶伎楽
第112窟南壁

65

77. **侍從菩薩・舞樂**　　第159窟西壁
Bodhisattvas and Musicians　　cave 159
脇侍菩薩　舞楽　　159窟西壁

78. 嫁娶圖　　榆林窟第25窟北壁
Scene of Marriage (Yu-lin Grottoes) cave 25
嫁娶図　　榆林窟25窟北壁

晚唐、五代、元代
Late Tang, Five Dynasties and Yuan Dynasty
晚唐、五代、元代

79. **近事女**　　第17窟北壁　　晚唐
Female Attendant　　cave 17
近侍女　　17窟北壁　　晚唐

80. **張議潮統軍出行圖（局部）**
第156窟南壁　　晚唐
General Zhang Yichao Going Outing
(section)
cave 156

張議潮統軍出行図（局部）
156窟南壁　　晚唐

81. **各族各國王子**
第98窟東壁　　五代
Heads of Various Nationalities
and Countries　　cave 98

各族各国王子
98窟東壁　　五代

83. **辯才天**　　第3窟北壁　　元代
Sarasvati　　cave 3
　　辯才天　　3窟北壁　　元代

82. **婆藪仙**　　第3窟北壁　　元代
Vasu　　cave 3
　　婆藪仙　　3窟北壁　　元代

多姿的彩塑

•

Various Painted
Sculptures

•

多様な彩塑

1. 交腳彌勒菩薩
   第275窟西壁　　北涼
   Cross-legged Maitreya
   cave 275
   交腳弥勒菩薩
   275窟西壁　　北涼

2. **彌勒佛龕**
第268窟西壁　　北涼
Maitreya in a Niche
cave 268

弥勒仏龕
268窟西壁　　北涼

3. 禪定佛
   第259窟　　北魏
   Buddha in Dhyana
   cave 259

   禅定仏
   259窟　　北魏

4. 菩薩
   第248窟中心柱　　北魏
   Bodhisattva　　cave 248
   菩薩
   248窟中心柱　　北魏

5. 彩塑一鋪
第432窟中心柱東向龕　　西魏
A Group of Painted Sculptures
cave 432

彩塑一組
432窟中心柱東龕　　西魏

7. 阿難
   第427窟中心柱西龕　　隋代

   Ananda　　cave 427

   阿難
   427窟中心柱西龕　　隋代

6. 迦葉
   第427窟中心柱南龕　　隋代

   Kasyapa　　cave 427

   迦葉
   427窟中心柱南龕　　隋代

8. 迦葉・菩薩・天王
第322窟正龕北　初唐
Kasyapa, Bodhisattva and Lokapala　cave 322
迦葉　菩薩　天王　322窟正龕北　初唐

9. 天王　第322窟　初唐
Lokapala　cave 322
天王　322窟　初唐

10. 彩塑一鋪　　第45窟　　盛唐
A Group of Painted Sculptures　　cave 45
彩塑一組　　45窟　　盛唐

11. 阿難・菩薩・天王
第45窟龕南側 盛唐

Ananda, Bodhisattva and Lokapala
cave 45

阿難 菩薩 天王
45窟龕南側 盛唐

12. 菩薩 第45窟龕北側 盛唐
Bodhisattva cave 45
菩薩 45窟龕北側 盛唐

13. 阿難　第45窟龕南側　盛唐
Ananda　cave 45
阿難　45窟龕南側　盛唐

14. 力士　第194窟龕南側　盛唐
Vijrapani　cave 194
金剛力士　194窟龕南側　盛唐

15. **大佛像頭部**
第130窟　盛唐
Head of the Great Buddha
cave 130

大仏像頭部
130窟　盛唐

16. 天王
　　第46窟西壁龕北側　　盛唐
　　Lokapala　　cave 46
　　天王
　　46窟西壁龕北側　　盛唐

17. 阿難・菩薩・天王　　第159窟龕南側　　中唐
Ananda, Bodhisattva and Lokapala　　cave 159
阿難　菩薩　天王　　159窟龕南側　　中唐

18. 迦葉二身　　18−1.第419窟　　隋代　　18−2.第45窟　　盛唐

Kasyapa　　18-1.cave 419　　Sui Dynasty　　18-2.cave 45　　High Tang

迦葉二体　　18−1.419窟　　隋代　　18−2.45窟　　盛唐

19. **彩塑菩薩**
第194窟龕內南側
盛唐

Bodhisattva
cave 194

彩塑菩薩
194窟龕內南側
盛唐

絢麗的絹畫
·
Gorgeous
Silk-paintings
·
絢麗たる絹画

1. 引路菩薩
Bodhisattva as Guide
of Souls
引路菩薩

2. 觀世音菩薩
Avalokitesvara
観世音菩薩

3. 耕作・生衣・婚娶
   Ploughing, Growing Clothes
   and Marriage
   耕作・生衣・婚娶

4. 男剃度圖
   Tonsure of the Men
   男剃度図

5. 女剃度圖

Tonsure of the Women

女剃度図

6. 觀音經變
   Illustration of
   Avalokitesvara-sutra
   観音経変

7. 女供養人及童子
Female Donor and Child
女供養者および童子

8. 男供養人
Male Donor
男供養者

9. 男供養人頭像
Head of Male Donor
男供養者頭像

10. 帝王出行圖
Emperor Going Outing
帝王出行図

11. 樹下説法圖
Buddha Preaching the Law
樹下説法図

93

12. 鹿女步步生蓮

Scene from the Story of the Deer-daughter

鹿女步步生蓮

13. 藥師淨土變（局部）　Paradise of Bhaisajyaguruvaiduryaprabhasa (section)　薬師浄土変（局部）

14. 乘象入胎

The Conception of the Buddha

乘象入胎

15. 九龍灌頂

The Washing of the
New-born Prince

九龍灌頂

16. 燃燈佛授記・太子遊觀見三苦
Dipamkara's Prediction; Old Age,
Sickness and Death
燃灯仏授記・太子遊観
見三苦

18. 天王
Lokapala
天王

17. 深山辭別
Farewell in the Mountain
深山辞别

19. 行道天王

Vaisravana on His Way
Across the Water

行道天王

100

21. 金剛力士
Vajrapani
金剛力士

20. 金剛力士
Vajrapani
金剛力士

渾樸的磚畫
•
Simple Paintings
on Bricks
•
質樸なれんが画

1. 奔龍
Running Dragon
奔龍

2. 胡人引駝
Foreigner Leading Camel
胡人ラクダ引き

秀勁的書法

·

**Elegant and
Forceful
Calligraphies**

·

端麗な書道

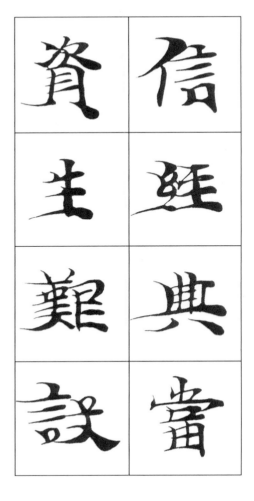

1. 隸書・大般涅槃經
Official-script: Mahaparinirvana-sutra
隷書・大般涅槃経

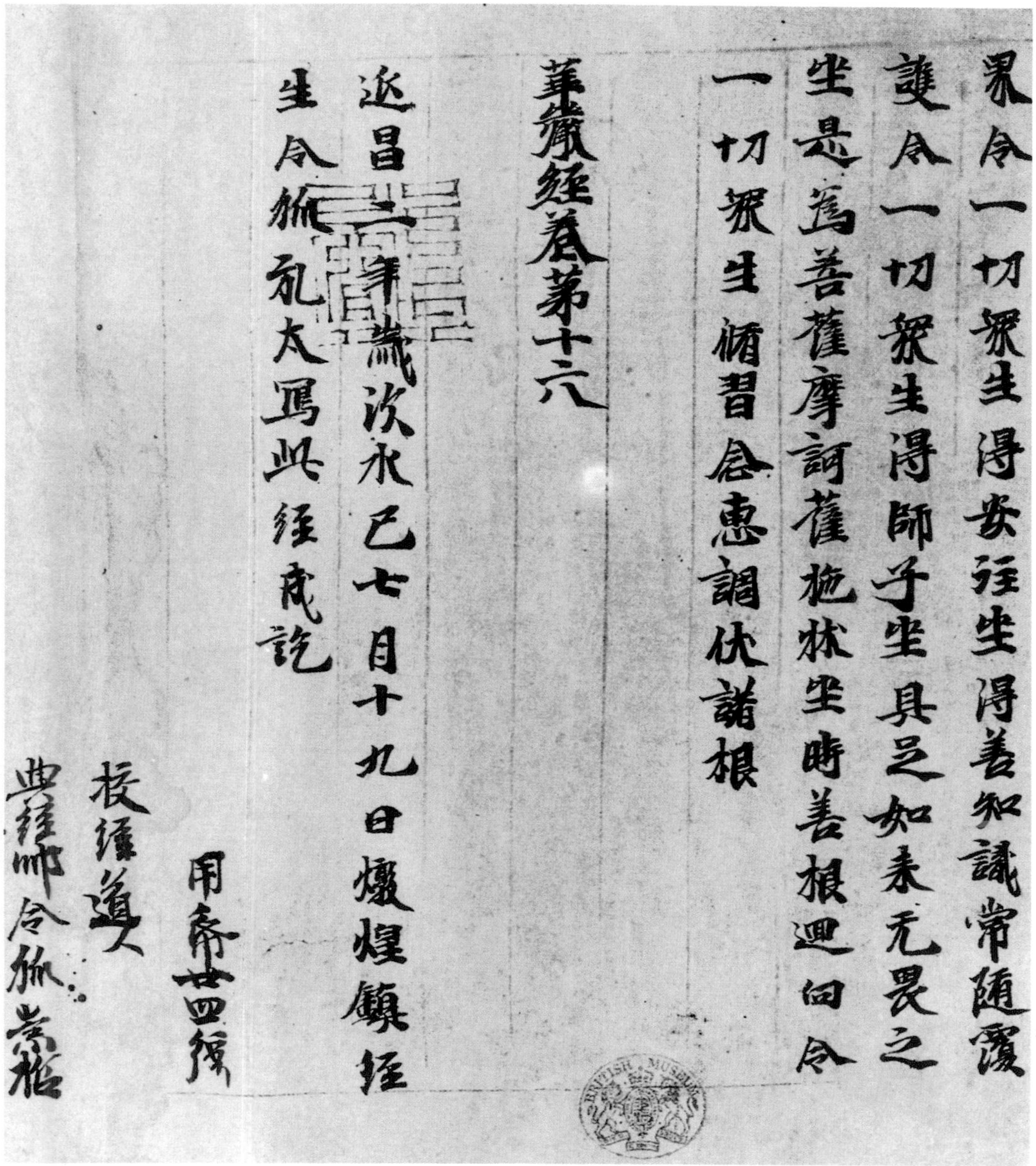
衆令一切衆生得安住生得善知識常隨覆
護令一切衆生得師子坐具足如來无畏之
坐是爲菩薩摩訶薩施林坐時善根迴向令
一切衆生脩習念惠調伏諸根
華嚴經卷第十六
延昌二年歲次癸巳七月十九日燉煌鎮經
生令狐礼太寫此經成訖
用帋廿四張
校經道人
典經師令狐崇哲
BRITISH MUSEUM

2. 楷書・華嚴經

Regular-script: Buddhavatamsaka-sutra

楷書・華厳経

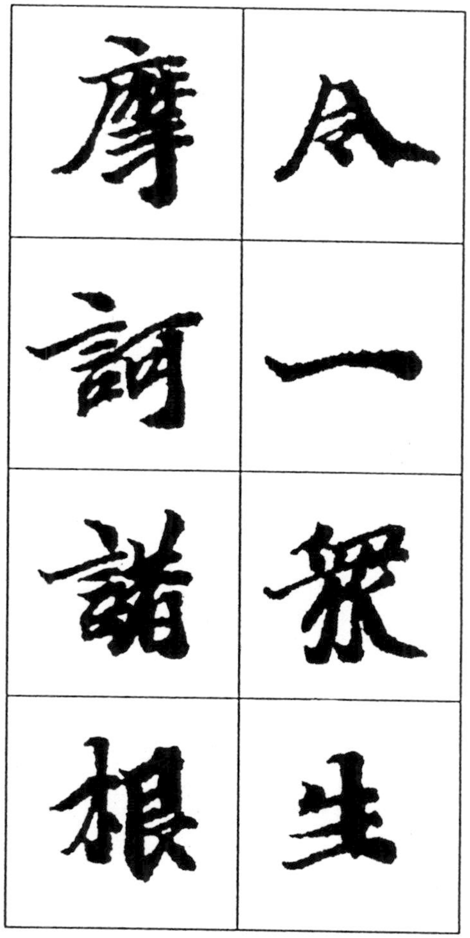
令
一
眾
生
摩
訶
諸
根

深義雖有篤信白衣檀越敬重佛法而諸弟
子演說經法貪為利養不為涅槃佛涅滅度
當知是法不久住復次善男子若佛涅滅出
浮阿耨多羅三藐三菩提已有諸弟子解甚
深義復有篤信白衣檀越敬重佛法彼諸弟
子凡可演說不貪利養為求涅槃佛雖滅度
當知是法久住於世復次善男子若佛滅出
得阿耨多羅三藐三菩提已雖有弟子解甚
深義復有篤信白衣檀越敬重佛法而諸弟
子多諸諍訟子猶是非佛復浬槃富如是法
不久住復次善男子若佛初出浮阿耨多
羅三藐三菩提已有諸弟子解甚深義復有

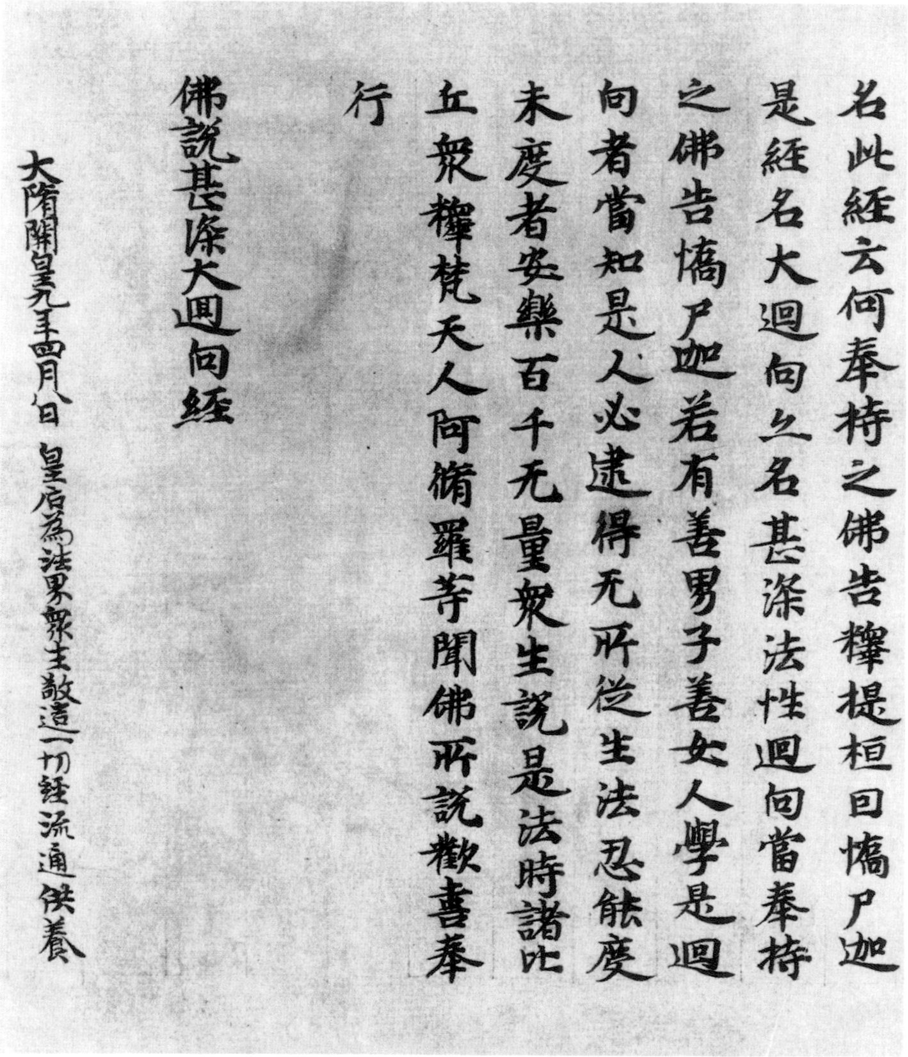

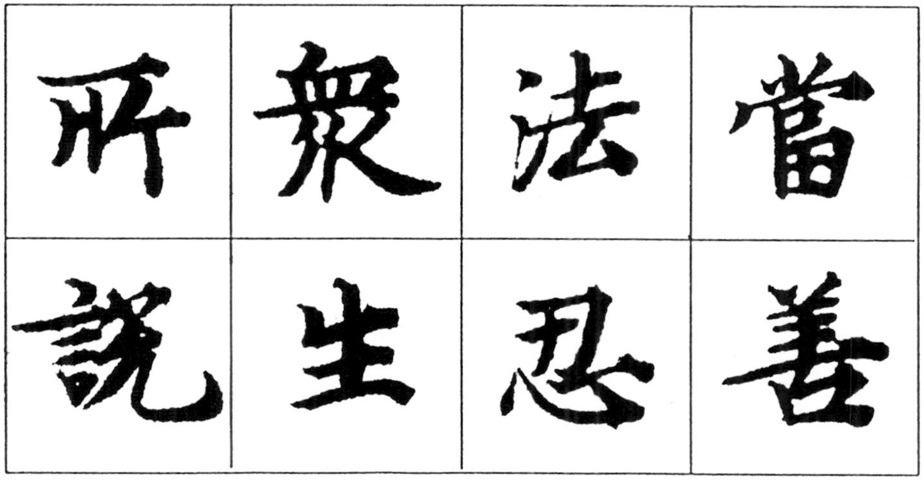

名此経云何奉持之佛告憍曰憍尸迦
是経名大迴向亦名甚深法性迴向當奉持
之佛告憍尸迦若有善男子善女人學是迴
向者當知是人必逮得无所従生法忍能度
未度者安樂百千无量衆生說是法時諸比
丘衆糴梵天人阿術羅苐聞佛所說歡喜奉
行
佛説甚深大迴向経

大隋開皇元年四月八日　皇后為法界衆生敬造一切経流通供養

4. 楷書・佛說甚深大迴向經
Regular-script: Fo shuo shen shen da hui xiang jing
楷書・仏説甚深大迴向経

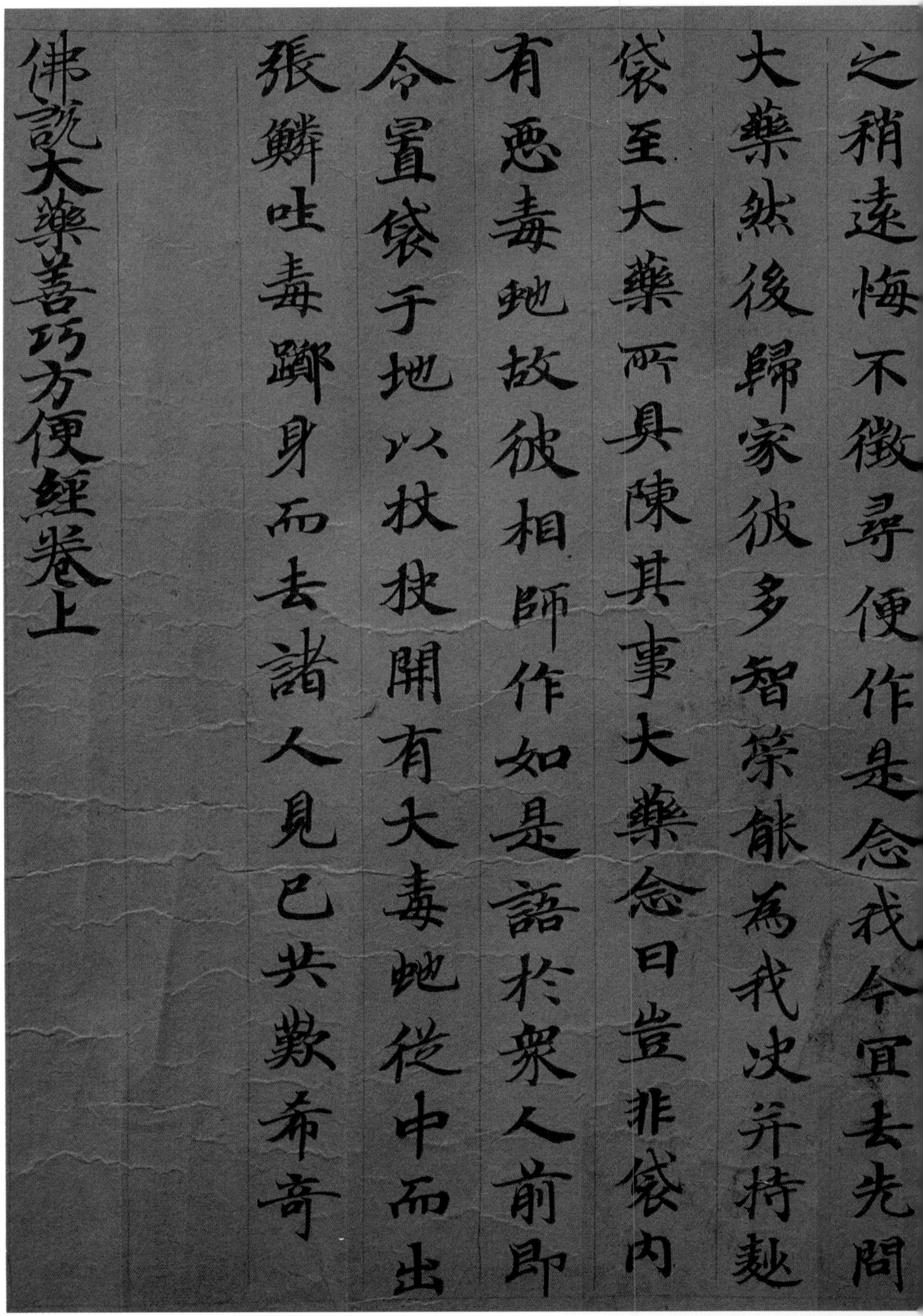

佛說大藥善巧方便經卷上

張鱗吐毒踦身而去諸人見已共歎希奇

令置袋于地以杖扙開有大毒虵從中而出

有惡毒虵故彼相師作如是語於眾人前即

袋至大藥所具陳其事大藥念曰豈非袋內

大藥然後歸家彼多智慧能為我決并持麨

之稍遠悔不徵尋便作是念我今宜去先問

5. 楷書・佛說大藥善巧方便經
   Regular-script: Fo shuo da yao
   shan qiao fang bian jing
   楷書・仏説大薬善巧方便経

自利于時國中善名流布王及諸臣寮庶之
類既聞知已作如是語我等有福感此勝人
共相保護不令枉横輙有侵欺
時有一人因向他方還来舊所在其城外池
邊歇息於皮袋中取麨而食忘不繫口餘處
旋行時有毒虵入於麨内其人既至不審觀
察繫袋持歸於城門外路逢相師告言男子
我觀汝顏命在須臾其人雖聞不將爲意

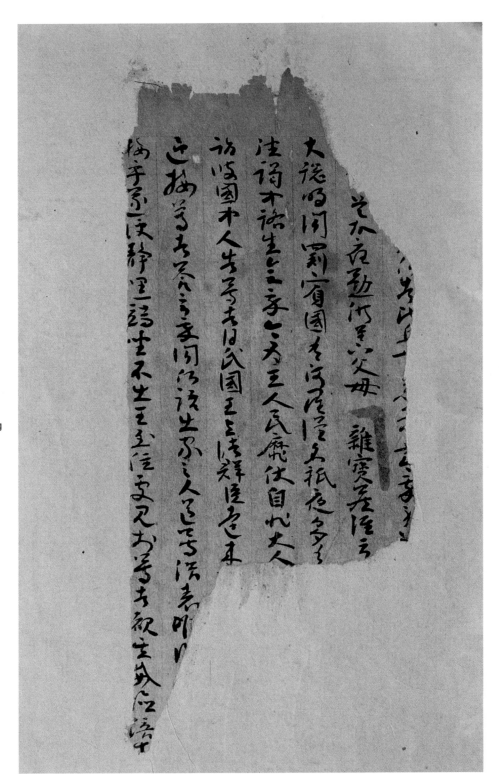

6. 草書・雜寶藏經
   Cursive hand: Za bao zang jing
   草書・雑宝蔵経

圖版說明

梁尉英　　楊　雄

輝煌的壁畫

北涼

1. 斗四藻井‧天宮伎樂　　第272窟

　　窟頂正中泥塑三重疊澀方井，層層內收。中心一朵大蓮花，岔角飾火焰紋半裸飛天，外四周忍冬雲紋。穹窿頂具有高遠的天際感。

2. 供養菩薩　　第272窟龕南

　　上下四行，每行五身，排列勻整。菩薩裸上身，披帛巾著天衣，或著長裙。席地而坐，或蹲踞，手勢臂姿各異。造型渾圓，格調樸實。

3. 供養菩薩　　第272窟龕北

　　與前圖相對位於西壁佛龕北側。菩薩沉靜溫婉。凹凸暈染，暖色渾厚，年久變色後粗獷豪放。西域風格濃厚。

4. 遊觀見老苦　　第275窟南壁

　　悉達太子出城遊觀，見到人生的生老病死之苦。此圖為老苦。悉達太子有頭光，從城門出來，遇見一老人。鬚髮蒼蒼的老人訴說人老的種種痛苦。

5. 毗楞竭梨王身釘千釘　　第275窟北壁

　　毗楞竭梨王執意求法，甘願身釘千釘。勞度叉左手握尖釘置王胸部，右手持鎚揚臂擊釘。王子平靜安然，勞度叉面相兇惡。畫風稚拙。

北魏

6. 三佛說法圖　　第263窟南壁

　　三佛分腿並立著，椎髻，偏袒袈裟，跣足。兩側供養菩薩，寶冠天衣長裙，體態優美。上部兩飛天巾帶回環繚繞，襯托出輕捷的飛動感。

7. 乘象入胎　　第431窟中心柱南向龕東側

　　此圖為佛陀八相成道的乘象入胎之相。鮮花飄飛的雲天中，大白象行進著。象背蓮花座上，坐著悉達太子，披長巾。華蓋兩側是翔龍。

8. 夜半逾城　　第431窟中心柱南向龕西側

　　此為佛陀八相成道的夜半逾城出家之相。悉達太子騎著白馬，騰空逾越城門。上有俯蓮華蓋。與前圖對稱，裝飾在佛龕兩側。

9. 天宮伎樂　　第248窟北壁

　　天宮前有欄楯。宮內伎樂，彈琵琶者，上身赤裸，下身著裙，披大巾；舉手於頭頂舞蹈者，身著天衣，披長巾。面相豐圓，蜂腰彎彎。白鼻白眼，光怪神秘。

10. 金剛力士　　第254窟西壁

　　金剛力士是執金剛杵護衛佛法的神祇。此三身力士，揮動手臂，蹲踞騰踏舞蹈著。舞姿大度，力度強烈。此為西涼樂中的健舞。

11. 九色鹿救溺人　　第257窟西壁

　　九色鹿救出了溺人。溺人發誓不泄露鹿的居所。王后讓國王捕鹿。國王懸賞捕鹿。溺人見利忘義，領著國王去捕鹿。九色鹿向國王陳說了溺人被救報恩之事。溺人受懲。救溺人和捕鹿分別繪於兩端，中間是故事的高潮和結局。

12. 沙彌守戒自殺之一　　第257窟南壁

　　這也是一幅橫卷式連環畫，依次描繪八個情節場面。此圖為長者送子出家和其子受戒被剃度為沙彌。

13. **沙彌守戒自殺之二** 第257窟南壁

此圖為高僧說戒、沙彌索食、少女求愛、沙彌守戒自刎。服飾為中西合璧，有漢裝、龜茲裝。

14. **沙彌守戒自殺之三** 第257窟南壁

圖為少女向父陳訴沙彌之死因和父向國王交納罰金。構圖簡煉，人物突出。以特徵性的禪窟屋舍為畫面單元的背景。

15. **沙彌守戒自殺之四** 第257窟南壁

圖為焚化沙彌和起塔供養。整體色彩均衡對稱，色調溫和濃麗，明暗暈染富有立體感。中西藝術風格都很明顯。

16. **薩埵捨身飼虎** 第254窟南壁

這個故事的壁畫此幅最早，其內容有：三王子山中遇餓虎，薩埵刺項和跳崖，餓虎啖食，國王和夫人抱尸痛哭、收取遺骨起塔供養。

17. **薩埵捨身飼虎（局部）** 第254窟南壁

此為餓虎啖食。構圖別具一格，單幅畫面中交織着不同時間的諸事。核心情節餓虎啖食，場面大，且居中，突出了主題。

18. **尸毗王割肉貿鴿** 第254窟北壁

餓鷹捕食鴿子。尸毗王用與鴿子等量的自身肉給鷹充饑，以救鴿命。中心是尸毗王，形體高大，神色安然。眷屬臣眾不忍目睹，或勸阻，或祈禱。構圖緊湊，暈染嫻熟，綫條流暢，着色厚暖。

西魏

19. **窟室（局部）** 第288窟主室

前部人字披頂，後部平棋頂。中心塔柱四面開龕，塑佛像和菩薩。圖為中心塔柱東向圓券龕，化生龕楣上方影塑千佛（殘）。窟室南北壁，上畫天宮伎樂，中畫千佛、說法圖，下飾三角垂幔。

20. **藻井·諸天神** 第249窟

覆斗頂，斗四藻井，井心大蓮花。西披（圖下部）畫手托日月的阿修羅和雷神、雨師、朱雀、烏獲。東披（圖上部）畫捧摩尼珠的力士和朱雀、開明等。這是佛道思想相融合在藝術上的表現。

21. **東王公** 第249窟北披

東王公居中（殘），身着大袖襦，坐在懸華蓋的四龍車上，紅袍造父持繮御車。前後有騎龍持節的方士。前有：耳出於項的羽人，頭似鹿、身有翼的飛廉，力士形、臂生羽的烏獲，人首鳥身的千秋。後有十三首人面虎身的開明。

22. **西王母** 第249窟南披

高髻的西王母，身著大袖襦，拱手而坐仙人駕御的鳳輦。輦上重蓋，後插旌旗。前有持節揚幡乘鷥仙人、烏獲、羽人、飛天。二方士騎鳳相隨於側。後有文鰩、白虎、開明。

23. **伏羲女媧** 第285窟東披

二力士弓步相向共舉蓮枝，上有摩尼珠。上部人面龍身獸爪、著大袖襦披帛巾者：右側伏羲，胸佩有三足烏的日輪，雙手擎規；左側女媧，胸佩有蟾蜍的月輪，一手持矩，一手提墨斗。

24. **說法圖** 第288窟北壁

金剛座上，主尊全跏坐，椎髻大耳，偏袒袈裟，內著掩腋衣。多層火焰紋背光，華蓋垂幔。兩側飛天和供養菩薩。構圖對稱，色艷厚暖。

25. **供養菩薩** 第249窟西壁北側

這六身菩薩，寶冠裙帔，裸上身。人體比例適度，程度不同地傾身突胯，蜂腰S型，體態嫵媚，俯首端莊，神情恬淡含蓄。

26. **飛天** 第285窟龕頂

這兩身飛天，頭戴菩薩冠，披帛巾，裸上身，下系長裙。臂勢手姿具有舞蹈性，輕盈飄揚的巾裙顯示着動律。

27. **飛天** 第249窟西龕頂

嫵媚的飛天，柔體頎長，白鼻白眼，秀雅端莊，肌膚玉潔，下身薄紗透體。一身吹奏竪笛，一身舉臂仰掌舞蹈。

28. **化生童子** 第285窟正龕楣

艷麗的蓮朵中，化生童子露半身，眉清目秀，滿臉稚氣，頭梳髻鬟。有的吹笙笛彈琵琶拍擊蜂腰鼓；有的應節拍掌，似在歌唱。左右對稱，綫條明快，色彩絢麗。

29. **天宮伎樂** 第249窟南壁

中間天宮為殿廡式，兩側為券形，前有曲折連續的欄楯。天宮伎樂，一身彈箜篌，兩身舞蹈。伎樂形象豪爽，畫面古樸典雅。

30. **天宮伎樂** 第288窟西壁

天宮伎樂，豐腴適度，面相條方，蠶眉柳眼，額貼花鈿，飾項圈手鐲，神情專注，撮唇吹氣之態和彈指按孔之勢，尤為寫實。

31. **天宮伎樂** 第288窟西壁

舞蹈的天宮伎樂，身軀側彎呈S狀。雖然下肢不露，但是身軀的動勢和重心，顯示出舞蹈動作的大度，踢踏鏗鏘。專心彈撥箜篌的，拇食二指控弦有力。

32. 金剛力士　　第249窟北壁

　　二金剛力士穿犢鼻褌。一身彈琵琶，扭身彎頭，抬腿作舞。一身蹲踏吹奏豎笛。獸頭藥叉披巾手舞足蹈。

33. 金剛力士　　第288窟中心柱南側

　　這兩身力士圓頭大腦，肢軀粗壯，蹲踏揮臂。披巾飄盪，尤顯豪獷。造型圓碩，誇張肌肉，力度感強，表現出一種強悍驍勁之風。

34. 護法諸天　　第285窟西壁正龕北側

　　上左爲鳩摩羅天，童子顏容，四臂，手持戟、葡萄、蓮花等，騎坐孔雀。上右爲毗那夜迦天，象首人身，手持三股金剛杵。下二身爲天王，儼若古代沙場武將。衣褶疏朗，曲綫流暢，立體感強。

35. 護法諸天　　第285窟西壁正龕南側

　　上爲二金剛力士，下爲二天王。侍處佛側，奉行護法。這裏金剛不怒目，天王是武夫，是寫實於世俗人物的造型。

36. 天界諸神　　第285窟西披

　　上部四肢博擊連鼓的是雷神。中部頭似鹿、身有翼的是飛廉。下部形似鳳凰的是朱雀，還有乘鸞仙女和飛天。中間化生童子舉托一盆鮮花。

37. 狩獵圖　　第249窟北披

　　重巒叠嶂。獵人騎馬追逐三只黃羊，舉槍欲投。黃羊奔命如飛。猛虎撲向獵騎。奔馬騰攀高山。獵人回首射虎。野牛驚懼，引頸張望。畫面氣氛驚恐緊張。

38. 禪廬・黃羊・老虎　　第285窟東披

　　草廬內苦修僧坐禪修道。林間兩只黃羊漫步着。草廬前三只黃羊停足豎耳，警惕地盯着老虎。老虎躡足走向黃羊。樹的描繪趨於寫實。

39. 禪廬・宰野猪・獵野羊　　第285窟南披

　　山峯櫛比，雲霧滾滾，廬內苦修僧入定。野羊靜臥，獵人迂回過去偷獵。一人持刀砍野猪，一手緊捉野猪尾巴，另一人刀插猪胸。

40. 作戰圖　　第285窟南壁

　　此圖爲《五百强盜成佛》中戰鬥場面。官軍有持盾步兵和鎧馬騎兵。强盜持盾弓劍矛斯殺。右部官軍凱旋，强盜被俘。造型生動細膩，是西魏壁畫中的傑作。

北周

41. 降魔變　　第428窟北壁

　　釋迦牟尼成道前與天魔波旬鬥法。中爲釋迦，全跏趺坐。左右爲魔軍，下部兩側爲波旬。左下三魔女以色相誘釋迦毀道。右下中間是釋迦法力使魔女變爲醜女。牛頭馬面者皆是魔兵，加害釋迦。此爲早期的經變畫，構圖單純。

42. 福田經變　　第296窟北披

　　《福田經》中說，種少許德，可收無量福。圖中畫了建佛寺、植果木、施醫藥、架橋樑、打水井等。佛經中的造船渡人，畫的是駱駝車。

43. 擲象・相撲　　第290窟人字披

　　此窟《佛傳》是鴻篇巨制，共87個畫面。圖爲裘夷要比武擇婿，在城樓觀看比武。象塞城門，釋迦擲象城外。比賽相撲，釋迦將另一人摔倒在地。

44. 射鐵鼓　　第290窟人字披

　　架懸七面圓鼓，一人騎馬監靶。右側四阿式建築內釋迦等三人彎弓射箭。前有四人觀看。釋迦一箭穿七鼓。

45. 藻井・裸體飛天　　第428窟西披

　　此窟後部平棋頂，繪斗四蓮花圖案，此爲其中的一幅。中心大蓮花，外飾卷雲紋、忍冬紋。外岔角各有一身裸體飛天，只披帛巾，同向旋轉飛行。這在敦煌藝術中是罕見的。

46. 飛天・菩薩　　第428窟南壁

　　四身半裸飛天，兩身彈奏琵琶箜篌，兩身舞蹈。供養菩薩，一身著掩腋衣，手提淨瓶，余三身裸上身，都穿波斯褲，腰結蔽膝，披巾垂地。身姿相同，手臂姿態各異。上下動勢相反，相映成趣。

47. 胡人馴馬　　第290窟中心柱西側

　　這幅是供養行列中的馴馬圖。胡人高鼻深目，一手執繮，一手執鞭，逼馬後退。高頭大馬後退揚起一蹄。靜中富動，生活氣息濃郁。

隋代

48. 中心塔柱　　第303窟

　　中心塔柱宏偉壯觀。正方體台座，上層四面各開一龕，塑佛和弟子等，浮塑龕樑和蓮柱，彩繪菩薩化生童子和圖案。台座承托七級倒塔，最下級塑仰蓮和龍。上六級原有影塑千佛。

49. 三兔蓮花藻井　　第407窟

　　這是有名的三兔蓮花飛天藻井。井心奔逐的三兔共有三只耳朵。三耳呈三角形，圍以圓形蓮花，繞以一周飛天。色彩豐富，描繪工細。此爲隋代藻井圖案的傑作。

50. 須達拏本生　　第419窟東披

葉波國太子須達拏樂善好施。外道求其國寶白象，他慷慨施予。國王大怒，將其驅逐出國。須達拏一路上將車馬衣服施盡，婆羅門乞去兩個孩子出售，國王贖回孫子，迎太子回國。故事畫分三層，上層從右開始，中層從左向右，下層從右向左。共畫50多個場面。

51. 菩薩　第420窟西壁北側

菩薩肌膚的暈染，既使用我國傳統的渲染法，也使用西域的叠暈法，較好地表現了立體效果。這反映了藝術上積極探索的隋代特點。

52. 執拂天女　第62窟西壁

執拂天女衣飾華麗，頭面肌膚暈染細膩，眉目神情朦朧而生動。

53. 供養車馬·山林人物　第303窟東壁

供養車馬，是當時的風俗寫實。下圖的山巒、樹木、野獸、獵者，樸拙中不失生動。

初唐

54. 說法圖　第322窟南壁

此爲彌勒說法圖。主尊居中倚坐，上有飛天菩提寶蓋，前有熏爐菩薩供養。兩側菩薩秀麗，或執蓮花，或托玻璃碗。左右大體對稱，風格淡雅。

55. 菩薩·弟子　第57窟南壁

此爲初唐代表作之一。菩薩細眉長目，鼻直唇紅，肌膚潤澤，情態嫻雅。弟子眉清目秀，楚楚動人。

56. 文殊·聽法帝王　第220窟東壁

文殊師利坐高座，下爲前來聽法的帝王羣臣。

帝王戴冕旒、着袞衣、飾十二章，雙臂張開，昂首闊步。賦彩豐富而和諧。

57. 思維菩薩　第71窟北壁

此窟壁畫被烟熏黑，清洗後顯露出初唐佳作。此二身菩薩戴寶冠，梳高髻，一作深沉思維狀，一似在靜思中微微而動，體態健美。

58. 菩薩　第334窟龕頂北側

這是說法圖中的一組菩薩，背景爲茂盛的芭蕉與菩提樹。在一片綠色中，人物顯得肌膚白晳俊美，表情自然而生動。

59. 舞樂之一　第220窟北壁東側

這是《藥師經變》樂舞東側一段。舞蹈即著名的胡旋舞。樂隊13人，演奏箏、簫、竪笛、方響、篳篥、阮咸、橫笛等。

60. 舞樂之二　第220窟北壁西側

此爲《藥師經變》樂舞西側一段，亦爲胡旋舞。樂隊15人，演奏笙篌、答臘鼓、羯鼓、羯鼓、毛員鼓等。

61. 藻井·飛天　第329窟

藻井中心爲蓮花，花心呈五色轉輪。花外四身飛天於藍天白雲間翱翔。圍以卷草、方格等紋樣及垂角幔帷。周圍伎樂飛天12身。色彩變化豐富。此爲初唐的代表作之一。

62. 各國王子　第220窟東壁

維摩詰居士精通佛法，與問疾的文殊菩薩論辯。圖爲前來聽法的各國王子，面相、體型、膚色、衣飾等各具特色。

63. 羣臣　第220窟東壁

此爲上圖中的羣臣像。有的小心翼翼，有的落落大方，有的雙目炯炯，有的含光內視，性格各異。

64. 各族君長　第220窟東壁

這是隨文殊菩薩聽法的各族君長，膚色、民族、職業、年齡諸方面顯示出差別。

65. 馬夫·馬　第431窟西壁

馬夫抱着繮繩，交脚抱膝，埋頭沉入夢鄉。三匹馬靜立左右，健壯馴順。構圖對稱而有變化，綫描有粗細虛實之分，設色厚實濃重。

盛唐

66. 化城喻品　第217窟南壁

《化城喻品》說有一羣人要去取寶，但道路險惡。衆人走了一段後，畏難欲退。有一導師，化出一城，讓衆人休息，然後繼續前進。這一內容成了一幅傑出的山水人物旅行圖。

67. 胡商遇盜　第45窟南壁

《觀音經》中說，有一大商人，齎重寶過險路，因爲一心念觀音名號，所以遇賊得以解脫。圖中所繪顯然是當年絲綢之路的眞實情景。

68. 菩薩　第217窟北壁

這一組菩薩有供養者，有禮佛者，有聽法者；有跪、有坐、有站；有正面、有側面；素面朱唇，婀娜多姿；多袒身飾瓔珞披帛。構圖富於變化。

69. 菩薩頭像　第45窟龕內南側

這是在彩塑背後的菩薩像，雲冠高髻，秀眼長眉，面相豐腴，設色艷麗。

70. 弟子頭像　　第217窟龕內北側

這一弟子頭像造型爲唐畫中並不多見的長眉羅漢像，綫描與暈染都十分顯功力。細則每根眉毛睫毛一絲不苟，粗則皺紋、五官輪廓一筆而就。暈染之工細濃淡仍約略可見。

71. 飛天穿樓　　第217窟北壁

這是《阿彌陀經變》上方的一組畫。樓閣是阿彌陀淨土的寶殿。天空的樂器不鼓自鳴。飛天從樓閣中悠然而過，飄然而起。祥雲裊裊，仙樂陣陣。

72. 男剃度圖　　第445窟北壁

儀仗王率大臣、太子、王后、宮女等八萬四千人追隨彌勒出家學道。此爲國王大臣等男子剃度圖。

73. 女剃度圖　　第445窟北壁

王后率宮娥彩女出家。比丘尼持刀削髮，被剃者雙手合十。侍者捧篋器以承落髮，雙眼緊盯主人的光頭。帷帳中等待剃髮者，有的虔誠，有的回首而視，亦有詢問的。

中唐

74. 舞樂圖之一　　第154窟北壁

樂隊坐平台上，舞者則於小橋上施展技藝。樂隊八人，第一排擊羯鼓、長鼓，第二排奏筌篌、琵琶、橫笛，後排一人擊拍板。

75. 舞樂圖之二　　第154窟北壁

此爲上圖之另一部。樂隊亦爲八人，前排三人吹笙、簫、排簫，中排四人奏篳篥、橫笛、拍板、執鈴。

76. 反彈琵琶伎樂　　第112窟南壁

反彈琵琶伎樂置琵琶於腦後，左腿獨立，吸右腿，展身向右，且奏且舞。飛動的舞帶提示了瞬間完成的動作，前移的重心又預告下一個招式。舞姿優美。

77. 侍從菩薩・舞樂　　第159窟西壁

圖爲文殊下的侍從菩薩和舞樂。有牽獅的昆侖奴、侍從跟隨的大菩薩、捧供器的供養菩薩。特別生動的是天人奏樂，且行且奏。吹笙者大腳趾打着節拍。

78. 嫁娶圖　　榆林窟第25窟北壁

佛經中說，彌勒之世，女子五百歲出嫁。圖中所畫却爲當時世俗的嫁娶圖。座上客人有藏有漢，新郎吐蕃裝，新娘漢裝。沿襲武則天時遺留的風俗禮節"男拜女不拜"。

晚唐・五代・元代

79. 近事女　　第17窟北壁　　晚唐

近事女即在家受佛教八戒的女子。此圖在洪䛒像右側，爲晚唐的精品。樹掛挎袋。近事女執杖托巾，梳雙髻，穿圓領缺胯長衫，腰束帶。臉型豐腴，裝束爲晚唐時式。綫描流暢，暈染細緻，設色層次豐富。

80. 張議潮統軍出行圖（局部）　第156窟南壁　晚唐

張議潮爲晚唐統一河西十一州的功臣。張議潮出行圖爲敦煌壁畫中的傑作。全圖長八米多，畫人馬百余。有軍樂、歌舞、儀仗，有子弟軍，有持節軍將，有輜重和行獵隊等。張議潮白馬紅袍，正欲揚鞭過橋。

81. 各族各國王子　　第98窟東壁　　五代

位於維摩詰下方聽法各族各國君長，前兩組或爲當時南方諸國的君長及隨從，後爲西域各族各國君長。冠型有皮帽、氈帽、山形冠、紅氈高帽、綉花錦帽、翻沿帽、搭耳帽等。

82. 婆藪仙　　第3窟北壁　　元代

婆藪仙原爲外道。早期石窟中的婆藪仙多作婆羅門像。此婆藪仙高髻蓮花冠，鬚眉拂然，穿交領大袖袍，是中原大仙的形象。

83. 辯才天　　第3窟北壁　　元代

辯才天又稱功德天，管國家安泰及個人福德。圖中天女戴花釵冠，飾巾幗，穿雲肩羽袖大帶裙襦，一手持蓮花，完全是漢式打扮。

多姿的彩塑

1. 交腳彌勒菩薩　　第275窟西壁　　北涼

這是現存早期最大的彌勒塑像。三角背光，化佛冠，飾瓔珞，披帛巾，下著裙。造型洗煉，交腳端坐，穩定持重。兩側塑雙獅。

2. 彌勒佛龕　　第268窟西壁　　北涼

圓券龕內塑交腳彌勒佛，宋代補塑頭部，螺髻，偏袒袈裟。龕頂畫蓮花，正壁畫佛光，兩側壁畫供養菩薩。火焰紋龕楣，希臘式柱頭。

3. 禪定佛　　第259窟　　北魏

跌坐禪定佛，椎髻，面相方闊，沉思入化。造型灑脫嚴整。陰刻綫衣紋隨勢自然起伏。

4. 菩薩　　第248窟中心柱　　北魏

菩薩清秀，神情端莊。儉裝無華，肌膚玉潔，充分表現了女性美。後人補修，未損原形。

5. 彩塑一鋪　　第432窟中心柱東向龕　　西魏

　　夯形龕，雙龍首龕樑，火焰紋身光。主尊善跏坐，外着大袖袍，內着僧祇支，挽結。二菩薩粗碩，神情靜謐，寶冠，披巾著裙。色彩豐富，格調明快。

6. 迦葉　　第427窟中心柱南龕　　隋代

　　迦葉是佛的弟子，少欲知足，修頭陀行。雙手合十，恭立佛側。形容枯槁，青筋暴突，面部棱角分明，目光炯炯，微現笑容。造型老成持重，很有內在活力。

7. 阿難　　第427窟中心柱西龕　　隋代

　　阿難也是佛的弟子，長於記憶，稱為"多聞第一"，雙手合十，恭侍佛側。肌膚豐實，衣着儉樸。藝術家賦予英俊少年的外相和氣質。神情專注，矜持瀟灑。

8. 迦葉·菩薩·天王　　第322窟正龕北　　初唐

　　迦葉清癯體健，通肩袈裟，足登雲頭履。菩薩身材修長，花冠垂帶，霞披系裙。天王戎裝，盔鎧戰裙蔽體，長靴護腿，腳踩地神。

9. 天王　　第322窟　　初唐

　　此為上圖的天王，濃眉大眼，目光有神，八字鬍，山羊鬚，嘴張含笑。神態堅毅豪爽，顯露出耿直忠厚的胸懷，是寫實傳神的傑作。

10. 彩塑一鋪　　第45窟　　盛唐

　　平頂敞口龕，塑像七身，體態各異，個性明朗。主尊正襟危坐，溫和慈祥。迦葉老態深沉，襟懷坦盪。阿難年少穎悟，敦實憨厚。菩薩婷婷玉立，秀外慧中。天王戎裝革裹，金剛怒目。

11. 阿難·菩薩·天王　　第45窟龕南側　　盛唐

　　此為上圖的局部。阿難年青持重，菩薩溫情，天王兇猛。但三者又是一個和諧的總體，同侍於佛側，神情相應，就連手臂的高低起伏也無不與主尊內在配合。

12. 菩薩　　第45窟龕北側　　盛唐

　　這尊菩薩上身全裸，飾以瓔珞披帛。高髻、蛾眉、紅唇，身段婀娜，肌膚柔軟，手臂修長，神態端莊溫情。她的形象是人間眷戀有情的嬌宮娃。

13. 阿難　　第45窟龕南側　　盛唐

　　佛的小弟子阿難，完全是一個年青英俊的小和尚。身體微扭作S形，嘴唇的棱角與眉眼的曲線，顯示出年輕、幼稚、單純。

14. 力士　　第194窟龕南側　　盛唐

　　這身佛教護法力士兩眼圓睜，張口怒喝，赤身露體，赤手空拳。他的力量充分表現於全身堅韌結實的肌肉上。

15. 大佛像頭部　　第130窟　　盛唐

　　大佛像高達26米，僅頭部高就7米。窟內觀者仰視會覺得頭面小。藝術家適當增大頭部體積，誇張面部五官，強調五官之間的過渡，利用明窗光綫加強面部造型。

16. 天王　　第46窟西壁龕北側　　盛唐

　　這身天王甲冑嚴身，作憤怒像。四肢多屈以成勢，有一股強大的力量表現於通身上下。相反，地神則似筋疲力竭。

17. 阿難·菩薩·天王　　第159窟龕南側　　中唐

　　此為吐蕃時期彩塑中的精品。阿難是一個虔心侍立的小和尚。菩薩身體S形，面相豐腴而略方，兩眼角上翹，服飾彩繪精緻細膩。天王盔甲式樣大約取材於吐蕃軍隊。

18. 迦葉二身　　18—1. 第419窟　　隋代
　　　　　　　　　　　18—2. 第45窟　　盛唐

　　這是兩個時代的迦葉造像。隋塑是飽經風霜的苦行僧。盛唐的則是飽覽人世變幻的哲人，超然深邃。

19. 彩塑菩薩　　第194窟龕內南側　　盛唐

　　這身具有女性美的男性菩薩，素面如玉，豐肌秀骨。圓領羅衣，飾以團花卷草等圖案，腰帶輕束，披帛繞臂，從衣紋可看出絲綢的質感。這是盛唐彩塑的精品。

絢麗的絹畫

1. 引路菩薩

　　紫雲霓霧中，具有女性美的男性引路菩薩，衣飾繁縟華貴，一手持手爐，一手舉彩幡，腳踩蓮朵，飄然而前行。身着大袖襦的婦人（亡靈）虛空隨行。盛唐富麗之畫風炳然。

2. 觀世音菩薩

　　這是天復十年（910年）的絹畫。觀世音菩薩，眉目疏朗，小鼻櫻口，大耳垂璫。頭戴化佛冠，瓔珞項飾繁複，短裙褲褶，跣足。右手持淨瓶，左手捻柳枝。構圖對稱，造型豐滿。綫條流利，色彩艷麗。唐風不減。

3. 耕作·生衣·婚娶

　　這是描繪彌勒淨土世界的樂事：農夫鞭牛耕作，寓示"一種七收"，架上掛着衣布，表示"樹上生衣"；帳幔內婚娶儀式，表示人壽無量，女子五百歲才出嫁。此畫實是唐代社會風情畫。

4. 男剃度圖

彌勒在華林園龍華樹下說法超度眾生。儀仿王削髮受度。侍者托盤承接落髮，抱水罐給王洗沐。四大臣恭侍。馬夫握韁牽鞍馬靜候。

5. 女剃度圖

此圖描繪的與前圖共爲一事。儀仿王王后公主宮女也落髮出家。圖爲僧尼給王后剃髮。公主宮女恭立合十陪候。王后乘坐的攢尖頂彩轎停放在地，轎夫站立等候。筆法細膩，描繪寫實。

6. 觀音經變

主尊六臂觀音，面相男性，戴化佛冠，全跏坐蓮台。一面六臂。上二手，右托月（內有三足烏），左托日（內有蟾蜍）。下二手，左持淨瓶，右持念珠。兩側爲救諸苦難：墜山、拘監、遇蟲獸、遭戮、逢雹、火燒。

7. 女供養人及童子

此爲前畫中的供養人，婦孺皆爲平民服裝。婦人虔誠虛掌合十。童子稚憨，披髮，短袍長褲，應景作戲合掌，分腿而立。

8. 男供養人

此亦爲前畫的局部。前跪年長者，舉手爐，後跪青年人，捧供品，都穿窄袖長袍，頭戴展脚幞頭，腰繫帶。這裏的供養人不是公式化的人物示意圖像，已是個性化的人物寫實肖像。

9. 男供養人頭像

此像雖殘，但頭部大形猶存，神韻尚在。仍不失爲上乘之作。面相方闊，濃眉高挺，鼻平抿唇，鬍鬚剛勁，立耳剛直，尤其臥魚眼黑珠中正，睛白無邪。一頂方正的展脚幞頭更托出人物的豐彩氣質。

10. 帝王出行圖

羽葆下，帝王戴寶冠，簪白筆。袞服兩襟對稱地上飾日（三足烏）月（蟾蜍），中飾青龍，左下飾卍字，右下不清。文臣儒將侍隨。人物造型兼有胡漢之風。

11. 樹下說法圖

菩提華蓋下，佛全跏坐在彌漫着鮮花的金剛座上，身着田相袈裟。兩側比丘菩薩聽法。構圖嚴謹，描繪入微，色彩輝煌，造型豐碩，是爲唐作精華。

12. 鹿女步步生蓮

南窟仙人河邊便溺，母鹿飲水受孕，生鹿女。鹿女去向北窟仙人借火種，每個脚印上長出朵朵蓮花。綫條粗實，逸筆草草，形象簡括。

13. 藥師淨土變（局部）

曲欄寶台上，藥師三尊站立着。中尊藥師佛，螺髻，右手捏藥丸，左手作與願印。左脇侍日光遍照菩薩，捧盤，內盛鮮花，右脇侍月光遍照菩薩，雙手蓮花合掌。台下一女子乞願。

14. 乘象入胎

摩耶夫人熟睡，夢見天空中童子乘象而來，入左脇，因此生悉達太子。朵雲上圓輪內，童子跪坐象背的俯蓮座上，虛掌合十。二侍童合十跪着，稚氣十足。

15. 九龍灌頂

摩耶夫人在無憂樹下腋生悉達太子，九龍吐清淨的溫涼二水沐浴太子。圖中胖乎乎的太子，站在俯蓮座的仰蓮盆內。宮女圍立侍俸着。畫風樸實。

16. 燃燈佛授記·太子遊觀見三苦

上圖爲燃燈佛對儒童摩頂授記。下圖爲悉達太子出遊四門，看見病苦老苦死苦的情景。病榻上，扶坐着一病人。戴帷帽的老婦人被小兒攙扶着。山丘上陳屍一具，雲朵上一人（亡靈）跪拜西天。繪王城一座。

17. 深山辭別

悉達太子出家修道，夜半乘白馬與車匿逾城而至深山。車匿和白馬回歸，太子坐巨石上，把寶瓔奇珍交車匿。車匿掩面流涕。白馬跪地吻太子脚。難捨難別之情表現得淋漓盡致。

18. 天王

天王怒目，雙手持握金剛寶劍，勇武威嚴。捲髮寶冠，鎧甲被體，脚踏呲牙咧嘴的地神。綫描暢達，圖繪細膩，誇張得體。

19. 行道天王

豎眉立目的天王，峨峨寶冠，鎧甲戎裝，執持戟矟，威風凜凜。神將天神擁侍隨行。遠山連綿，江河滾滾，雲騰霧罩，意境恢宏壯闊。

20. 金剛力士

此身金剛是老年之容，雙手托持金剛針，裸體披飾巾帶。肌肉勾勒簡潔利落，廖廖綫條，既刻畫出塊塊肌肉的豐滿和顏容神情的威嚴，又是棉裏藏針，內隱堅骨硬挺，形神統一，表現出陽剛之美。

21. 金剛力士

此身金剛力士，左手作金剛拳，右手垂持金剛杖。造型、綫描、神韻等遜於前者。

渾樸的磚畫

1. 奔龍

　　敦煌三危山老君堂出土。五代的清磚面上模製突起的二奔龍。S型龍體，彎曲自如。一昂首一回頭，奔騰飛躍。動態逼真，豪壯奔放。具有古拙渾厚之美。

2. 胡人引駝

　　敦煌佛爺廟唐墓出土。胡人波斯裝，一手執繮牽駝，一手拄持手杖跋涉着。駱駝長脖高揚，昂首翹尾，馱載着貨物緩步跟隨。造型簡括，富於生活氣息。

秀勁的書法

1. 隸書·大般涅槃經

　　此為北魏時代的抄卷，字迹為寫經體，字形扁平方折，筆畫波磔分明，針芒起筆，頓逆凝珠收筆，曾頭其脚，結體勻實。剛柔相濟，相得益彰。

2. 楷書·華嚴經

　　此件為北魏延昌二年（513年）的筆迹。漢隸的波磔餘韵猶存，魏晉的筆畫平正之風已具。由隸而楷的演變踪迹卓然可見。

3. 楷書·大般涅槃經

　　此件為北周保定元年（561年）的寫卷。楷體內蘊隸書行書之味。筆畫豐肥，轉折圓潤，剛用柔顯。結體密實，方圓統一，剛柔中和雅靜。

4. 楷書·佛說甚深大迴向經

　　此件是隋代開皇九年（589年）的寫經。筆法拘謹，但力量彌滿，方折圓實，端正工穩，字迹凝重，體豐骨勁，神韵尚佳。

5. 楷書·佛說大藥善巧方便經

　　全帙字字若珠璣，秀麗纖巧。方正勻稱，一筆一畫如刀削刻。筆力蒼勁，筆法諳熟，筆勢挺拔利落，神韵典雅。由此可見我國書法藝術的唐時風采。

6. 草書·雜寶藏經

　　此件為聽講經時的筆錄。行草溶於一爐，簡約流便，綽約多姿，活潑灑脫。筆畫省減，因字生變，措置裕如，筆趣橫生。氣貫意連，豪放闊落。

封面　隨行婦人

　　此為絹畫中《引路菩薩》的隨行婦人（亡靈）。面相豐圓，楊葉眉，柳葉眼，小鼻小嘴。頭飾拋家髻，身著大袖襦，長裙曳地，儀態端莊。豐腴為美的唐人審美情趣於此可得領略一二。

執筆：

楊　雄：《輝煌的壁畫》42—43
　　　　《多姿的彩塑》11—19
梁尉英：《輝煌的壁畫》1—41
　　　　《多姿的彩塑》1—10
　　　　《絢麗的絹畫》
　　　　《渾樸的磚畫》
　　　　《秀勁的書法》

書名題字　段文傑

Explanation of the Plates

Liang Weiying   Yang Xiong

RESPLENDENT MURAL PAINTINGS

North Liang (907-923)

1. Square ceiling and heavenly musicians
cave 272

The top of this cave is a three stories square ceiling, made of clay which decoed with a huge lotus in the center, surrounded by several semi-naked flying apsaras. These figures are all in clouds. The whole picture looks just like floating in sky.

2. Attendant Bodhisattvas   south niche   cave 272

Four lines of semi-naked bodhisattvas, five ones on each line standing orderly, in silk clothes or long skirts. Sitting on ground or squntting on their heels. Different gestures of their arms. But all of these images are simple and vivid.

3. Attendant Bodhisattvas   north niche   cave 272

Encounter with the former picture, located in the north niche of the west wall. With a style of western border areas, the bodhisattvas looks quite and gentle. The color fade yet quite rough.

4. The encounter with the old age
south niche   cave 275

Prince Siddhartha left his palace and see for the first time a man enfeebled by age. The picture shows the prince in nimbus was just encountering with an aged man who told the former varieties sufferings of the old.

5. Jataka of king Biliengjieli
north niche   cave 275

The king not afraid of being nailed, because he is decided to be a disciple of Buddha. The heretic Raktahsha's left hand with a sharp nail, his right hand with a hammer. Raktaksha's face is very fiendish, while king's quite calm. An odd and strange style.

Northern Wei (386-534)

6. A Triad of Buddhas preaching doctrine
south niche   cave 275

Standing in a line side by side, there buddhas are all in kasaya, their hair tied up and foots naked. Attendant bodhisattvas wearing coronets and draperies on both sides of them. Above them are two beautiful flying apsaras.

7. Conception of prince Siddhartha   cave 431

One of 8 pictures showing how the prince to attain Enlightenment. It is entitled 'Conception'. The prince in long draperies is ridding on a white elephant walking in sky. Color flowers and buddha's canopy and deva dragons are with him.

8. Siddharha crosses over the wall   cave 431

A white horse carrying the prince Siddhartha is crossing the city wall. Above them is a huge lotus umbrella. This is painted on the side wall of the niche.

9. Musicians in a heavenly palace
north wall   cave 248

Behind the gate of deva palace, there are deva musicians in skirts playing pipa or dancers wearing draperies. Well shaped faces slim bodies and white noses, they look some mysterious.

10. Vajrapani   west   cave 254

This three bodies figure holding vajra is a god who protect Buddhism. The strong dance met with musical rhythm is of local features in the time of Western Liang.

11. Jataka of the Deer King   west   cave 357

A deer saved a drown man who promised he will never tell others where the deer hid. Queen asked his king to catch the deer. The drown being guide of king's hunters for the sake of his private interests caught the deer. Ironically, the drown was eventually punished by the king. Middle of the picture shows how the drown was punished.

12. Hetupratyaya of the Sramanera committing suicide for observing the Sila (1)

south wall   cave 257

This is also one of a series pictures showing a father supporting his son to receive Buddhist ordination of being a sramanera.

13. Hetupratyaya of the Sramanera committing suicide for observing the Sila (2)

south wall   cave 257

It shows that a master preaching silas, a sramanera asking food. He fell in love with a girl and finally he was suicide for the sake of observing the silas. It is interesting to note that their clothes have a combinational style of Hans and western minorities.

14. Hetupratyaya of the Sramanera committing suicide for observing the Sila (3)

south wall   cave 257

It shows a girl explaining to her father why the sramanera would suicide and her father offered a fare to the king. Images of these peoples occupy a large part of the picture which takes a typical meditation cave as its background.

15. Hetupratyaya of the Sramanera committing suicide for observing the Sila (4)

south wall   cave 257

Burning the sramaner's body and erecting a stupa for him. The color of the picture is well-distributed and symmetric with a suitable tone. It looks stereoscopic. A distinct artistic style of Sino-foreign paints.

16. Jataka of Prince Sudana

south wall   cave 254

This painting is comparatively old. The 3rd prince running into a hungry tiger, then he prinked hid neck and jumped off the cliff and finally was eaten by the tiger. King and queen are crying for their son. They are collecting his left bones and set up a stupa.

17. Jataka of Prince Sudana (details)

cave 254

A detail picture shows how the tiger ate the prince Sudana. Views of other things happened in different time being its background.

18. Jataka of king Sivi   north wall   cave 254

A hunger hawk is ready to eat a pigeon. King Sivi prefers to sacrifice his own body to save the bird. The king is the focus of the painting. Officials and relatives wouldn't like to see his misery. They persuade and pray for their king. By contrast, the king looks calm and peaceful.

Western Wei (535-556)

19. Shape of a cave (detail)   main hall   cave 288

Statute of bodhisattvas and buddhas are carved on the central column in this cave. In the east ward niche, are a part of a thousand buddhas carving. On the south and north walls, there are images of deva musicians and dancers on the upper line, a thousands buddhas preaching doctrines at the middle and triangle curtain at the bottom.

20. Square ceiling and deties   cave 249

Roof of the cave is a square ceiling decorated with a huge lotus. On the west wing (bottom of the picture) there are Asura holding sun and moon, god of thunder, rains, and scarlet bird etc. on the east wing (upper layer of the cave), vajra grasping pearls and scarlet bird, etc. These images reflecting a combination of Buddhist and Buddhist arts.

21. East-king-father   north   cave 249

The lord (middle, fragment) in robe with long sleeves, sits in a four -dragon-drawn chariot. The driver in red robe, after a alchemist ridding on a dragon. Front: a celestial being with big ears, wings, deer head, vajra-shaped body. Rear: an immortal with 13-heads and a tiger body.

22. West-queen-mother   south wing   cave 249

The queen whose hair tied up, in a robe with a big sleeves, joining hands, sits in a phoenix-cart drived by a immortal. There is a luxurious umbrella above her head. Colorful banners on the back of the chariot. Front: banner-holding immortal ridding a phoenix, winged man, flying apsaras before two alchemists. Rear: white tiger and other supernatural beings.

23. Fuxi and Nuwa   east   cave 285

Two vajras holding lotus and pearls stand on both sides. Above them is a celestial being in large robe with man-face, dragon body and beast claws. Right: god Fuxi, hanging a three foot bird symbolizing sun on his neck, his two hands grasping a gui (compasses). Left: god Nuwa, hanging a frog the symbol of moon, one hand grasping a jie (rule) and the other an inkmarker of carpenter.

24. Buddha preaching the law

north wall   cave 288

A big ears Buddha sitting on vajra seat, his legs crossed, hair tied up and kasaya covering one side of his body. Behind him are flaming a nimbus and canopy. Flying apsaras and an attendant bodhisattvas are around him. The whole picture emphasizes a spirit of order and harmonious.

25. Attendant bodhisattvas

northwest wall   cave 249

Six-bodies bodhisattva, putting on crown, a robe only covering a half of his body, naked beast. Big hipbone, slim body. Whole structure of the body looking fascinating and pretty.

26. Apsaras   cave 285

Two bodies goddes, wearing a bodhisatvas style crown, silk scarf and a skirt, breast naked. His moving hands and flying skirt tell you he is dancing.

27. Apsaras   west   cave 249

Pretty apsaras, thin body with white nose wears silk and satin skirt. She looks very dignified and graceful. One is playing flute, the other stretching arms and dancing.

28. Reborn children   middle niche   cave 285

From beautiful lotus flowers, out of a reborn boys' upper body. These children all have different delicate features. Some are blowing flute, playing pipa or bitting drums; some are likely singing. The whole picture are joyful and harmonious.

29. Deva Musicians in a heavenly palace

south wall   cave 249

Middle: a heaven palace, its left hand right wing are two archways, connected with a zigzag balustrade. One is playing konghou (a kind of old Chinese musical instrument.) The picture is simple and elegant.

30. Musicians in a heavenly palace

west wall   cave 288

The apsaras, body is not fat nor thin, with a square face and pretty eyes and eye brows. She wears some small ornaments like necklace and bracelet. Absorbed in playing a kind flute the image is very realistic.

31. Musicians in a heavenly palace

west wall   cave 288

Goddess in dancing, her s-shaped body, though being covered by skirt, the centre of her gravity shows the dancer is very strong. Another apsaras is absorbed in playing musical instrument called konghou.

32. Vajrapanis   north wall   cave 249

Two vajrapanis wearing trousers of national features. One is playing pipa, his body turning round, and one of his leg lifting showing he is in dancing. The other is blowing a bamboo flute. Some beast headed yaksas are dancing nearby.

33. Vajrapani   south   central pillar   cave 288

The two vajrapanis are all very strong and strength. Their round heads and sturdily built bodies are painted quite dramatically.

34. Devas   north west wall   cave 285

Left of the upper line: Jiumolotian, red face, four arms holding Ji (halberd), grape, lotus etc, is ridding on a peacock. Right of the upper: Pinayijatian, elephant-head and man-body, one hand holding a three-heads Chu (spear). Below: two vajras like ancient generals.

35. Devas   southwest wall   cave 285

Two vajras on the upper and two lokapalas on the below. They are all guards of Buddha. These vajras are not too fiendish as they were. Lokapalas were written after ancient soldiers.

36. Deieties   westwing   cave 285

Top: god of thunder beating drum. Middle: a deer-head, winged body goddess called Feiliang. Below: phonies-like Zhuqie (scarlet bird) goddess ridding birds and flying apsaras.

37. Scene of hunting   north   cave 249

The hills. Hunters ridding on horses after three goats, lifting their guns aimed at targets. Goat escaping desperately. A tiger jumping toward horses and made them frightened lifting their feet. Hunter ready to shot tiger. Several wild oxes by looking this scene in trembling.

38. Scene of dhyana   east wing   cave 285

An old monk sitting and undergoing ascetic pracing and precautions against invades from the tiger which is closing toward them. Those trees are painted as real.

39. Scene of dhyana   south   cave 285

Mountains and clouds, old monk sits in meditation. Hunter going silently toward these sleeping wild goats. A scene of killing boar. One's hand grasping the tie of the boar, the other pricking it with a knife.

40. Battle   south wall   cave 285

The picture of a battle field based on a story called "How 500 bandits attained bodhihood". Official army including infantrymen holding shield and cavalry ridding horses. Bandits take shields and swords.

Right: Officials army's victory. Bandits were captured. It is a master piece of mural paints in Western Wei period.

Northern Zhou (557-581)

41. Vanquishing Mara   North wall   cave 428

It is an illustration of story of how prince Shakyamuni defeat Mara before he attained the

Enlightenment.

Middle: Shakyamumi sitting crossed legs, army of Mara gathering around him. Below: Mara Pjapiyas. Left of below: three Maras lure Shakyamuni with their beauty. Right of below: Shakyamuni subjugated them. All of those having oxhead and horse face are soldiers of Mara. This kind of simple picture belong to those of early Buddhist story.

42. Illustration of Fu Tian Sutra

north   cave 296

The sutra teaches, everyone would gain endless fortunes if he/she had ever a little godliness. The picture gives several examples: building temples, planting trees, providing medicines, erecting bridges, drilling wells etc.

43. Throwing elephant and wrestling   cave 290

In the cave, there are 87 pieces of pictures consisting a large series illustrating a story of Buddha. King of Kasi would like to select a son in law throw a martial. Shakyamuni throwing an elephant out of the city gate and also defeating all challengers became the only winner.

44. Shooting iron-drums   cave 290

Setting up 7 round iron drums, one person riding horse is inspecting. Right: Shakyamuni and other two persons are all ready to let the arrows gone. Four men are watching, finally Shakyamuni's arrow hitting seven drums.

45. Naked apsaras in the square-ceiling

west   cave 428

On a flat ceiling, there are 4 square picture lotus. Centre: a large lotus, decored with cloud designs. Four outer corners is naked apsaras in silk clothing. This kind of pictures are rarely in Dunhuang.

46. Apsaras and bodhisattvas

south wall   cave 428

Four seminaked apsaras. Two are playing pipa and konghou, the other two are dancing. 4 attendant bodhisattvas: one's hand holding a rare bottle. The other three ones, waring Persian skirt-pants, naked breasts. Their body gestures are interesting.

47. Foreigner training steed   west   cave 290

On the picture, the foreigners having a big nose and blue eyes, his one hand is grasping reins, the other one whipping a horse to back, making its one leg lifting up. A realistic description of living scene.

Sui Dynasty (581-618 AD)

48. Central stupa-pillar   cave 303

A magnificent decorated pillar, square stage, four niches on each side of the 7 upper pagodas. Images of Buddha and his disciples are carved on them. Color painted bodhisattvas-reborn children. On the first stage of pagoda are carved lotus and dragons. There are total of 1000 statutes of buddhas.

49. Lotus-square-ceiling with three rabbits

cave 407

This ceiling is very famous. Three rabbits in running have three ears in total, forming a triangle. Surrounded by a round lotus and many flying goddess. Judging from its color and craftsmanship, it is a typical ceiling design of Sui dynasty.

50. Jataka of Sudana   east wing   cave 419

Prince Sudana is well known for his kindness and Dana. Once upon a time, a heretic asked him the white elephant which was considered as the national treasure. And the prince gave him. This made his father quite angry. The prince was then expelled out of his fatherland, yet he gave all he had, including his chariot,

horse, clothes, and even his two sons. Later, the kind took his grand son and Sudana back to his kingdom. Pictures of this stories including more than 50 scenes consisting 3 lines.

51. Bodhisattvas   northwest side   cave 420

Using techniques of Chinese traditional arts and that of western national arts, the bodhisattvas' masculars are very clear and has a effect of tri-dimension. This is a new artistic feature of Sui.

52. Attendant Goddess   west   cave 62

The goddess in luxurious and pretty clothes, her skin on face are beautiful and eyes are moving.

53. Cart, horse, forest and figures,   cave 303

Cart and horse are popular contents of painting at old time. Hills, forest, wild animals, hunters in this piece of paints are simple yet quite moving.

Early Tang Dynasty (618-907)

54. Buddha preaching the law

south wall   cave 322

This is Future Buddha Maitreya in preaching Buddhism. Middle: the Buddha, above him are flying goddess and bodhi umbrella. Front: incence-burner and attendant bodhisattvas beside him are pretty, some holding lotus, some lifting glass bowls. The style is elegant and it looks symmetric.

55. Boddhisattva and Disciples

south wall   cave 57

It is one of representative paintings in early Tang period. The bodhisattva was painted as a big eyes and long eye brow, big nose, red lip, with smooth skin. His disciples also looks pretty and admiring.

56. Manjusri and Emperor   east wall   cave 220

Sitting on a high stage, Manjusri is preaching for a king and his officials. The king wearing straw rin cape and 12 kind of ornaments, stretching his arms at riding forward with his chin up. The whole paints is harmonious and beautiful.

57. Meditating bodhisattva north wall cave 771

This is also a rare masterpiece painted in early Tang. It was once polluted by smoke. One of these two bodhisattvas wearing crowns with hair tied up, is in deep meditating, the other one is likely moved in thinking. They are all very shaped.

58. Bodhisattvas north cave 334

These bodhisattvas are parts of a series entitled Preaching Doctrine. Green BAJIAO and bodhitrees at the back of them making them more white and pretty and moving.

59. Orchestra (1)

northeast side cave 220

Illustration based in a story of Bhaisajyaguru or medician Buddha. The dance is well known as Huxuan Dance which is popular in the north west border area of China. There are 13 persons in total, including players of a lot of ancient Chinese vocal music instruments like Zhen, Xiao etc.

60. Orchestra (2)

northwest cave 220

Dance is the same as above section, say, Huxuan Dance. 15 persons in the band including players of different ancient Chinese percussion instruments like LA-drum, Jie-drum, Mayan-drum etc.

61. Apsaras in square-Ceiling cave 329

The center of the ceiling is a huge lotus like five-color-wheel. 4 goddess flying around the flower in the blue sky and white clouds decorated with smart designs of straws square etc. Beyond them are 12 deva musicians. It is a colorful paints in early Tang.

62. Princes from various countries

east cave 220

Vimalakirti was an specialist in Buddhist classics. In the picture, he was discussing Buddhism with Manjusri. Audiences including many princes of various countries with different physiques, skins and clothes.

63. Ministers east wall cave 220

This is a part of above picture. Officials listening to Vimalakirti have different facial expression of care, easy etc.

64. Heads of various nationalities

east wall cave 220

Accompanying with Manjusri, various leaders of different colors, ages, professions, nations are gathering here to listen to Vimalakirti's preaching.

65. Groom and steed west wall cave 431

A groom holding halter sits falling in sleep and dream. 3 horses standing silently beside their host. The picture is of symmetric and motion. Its artistic technique is good.

High Tang (618-907)

66. Parable of the illusory City

south wall cave 217

The picture was painted based on a classic story. A band of persons are on their way to find treasure and fortune. A lot of difficulties stop them. Then came a master. He makes a illusory city for their rest and go on travelling with his supernatural power. It is an excellent picture of landscape and persons.

67. Merchants encountering with bobbers

south cave 45

According to Valokitesvara Sutra, a rich merchant ever had a long trip carrying a lot of money with him. Because he kept on reciting the name of the bodhisattva. He was safe all the time even when he was encounting with a band of bandits. The picture is a realistic description of commercial situation on the ancient Silk Road.

68. Bodhisattva north wall cave 217

Among these bodhisattvas, there are worshipers, prayers and listeners, sitting, standing or kneeling. They showing their front faces or side faces, but all of their faces are white with red lips, priceless ornaments on their body which making them more graceful.

69. Head of bodhisattva south side cave 45

Located behind a color statute of a bodihasattva with a high crown and tied up hair, pretty eyes and eyebrows and a well shaped face.

70. Head of a disciple north cave 217

This kind of ling-eyebrow Arhat is an extraordinary example of arts in early Tang. The paints is very skillful especial in painting eyebrows and using color.

71. Apsaras north wall cave 217

A picture based on a story of Amitabha. The high building is the palace of the Buddha, musicial instruments in sky ring automatically. An apsaras is lying from afar across the palace. A beautiful scene.

72. Tonsure of the men north cave 445

An emperor leading his officials and relatives, 8400 persons in total, to follow Buddha Maitreya. The picture shows that situation of tonsue of these men.

73. Tonsue of the women   north wall   cave 445

The Queen leading crowds of concubines to receive silas. A nun's hand holding a knife to cut hair of disciple who put her hand in front of the breast. A servant lifting a basket to containing hair cut, watching the nun's head. Peoples in curtin are those who are waiting for having their hair cut.

Middle Tang (618-907)

74. Orchestra (1)   north   cave 154

Player of the instruments are siting on a stage, while dancers making performance on a little bridge. 8 members in the orchestra player of the first row: two drum player, the second row: players of konghou, pipa and vertical flute, rear: player of clappers.

75. Orchestra (2)   north   cave 154

Another part of the above picture. The orchestra consisting by 8 player in 3 rows.

Front: 3 players of sheng (reed pipa wind instrument), xiao (vertical bamboo flute) and paixiao. Middle: 4 players of whistle, clappers bell etc.

76. Dancer   south wall   cave 112

Standing a left leg, she dances and puts her two hands behind her head and plays a pipa. Flying clothes remind lookers that she is in dancing. A very beautiful gesture of the dancer.

77. Bodhisattva and musicians

cave 159

Manjusri and musicians are two heroes of the picture, followed by servant pulling a lion. Visiting great bodhisattvas and attendants bodhisattvas carrying offerings. Devas walking and playing musical instruments. A sheng-players foot shakes in harmous of music.

78. Scene of marriage

north wall   cave 25   Yuling Grotto

It was said in time of Maitreya women would be married after age of 500 years. Guests including Hans and Tibetans. The kowtowing bridegroom in Tibetan clothes in accordance with an old tradition while bride in 'Han' style.

Later Tang, Five Dynasties and Yuan Dynasty

79. Female attendant

north   cave 17   Later Tang

Female attendants are women receiving silas yet not being nuns. The picture is a treasure one in Later Tang. The attendant holding a stick and a towel, her hair tied up, wearing a long skirt with Later Tang style, a belt around her waist. A well-shaped face she has.

80. General Zhang Yichao on expendition (detail)

south wall   cave 156

The general was an official in Later Tang. The picture is really a masterpiece in Dunhuang. A length of 8 meters, it contains more than 100 figures of people and animals, including band of army, dancers, singers, generals and all kind of carts. General Zhang in red robe ridding a white horse was crossing a bridge.

81. Kings and princes of countries

Five Dynasty   east wall   cave 98

Leaders of various tribes and countries gathering together to listening the preaching of Ven Vimalakerti. They standing in 2 lines. Front: kings and their followers from south areas. Rear: kings of western areas. People wearing different hats.

82. Vasu

north   cave 3   Yuan dynasty

Vasu was usually painted as a Brahmanic herdtic in early grottoes. On this one, vasu with hair tied up, a lotus crown on the head, black eyebrows, wearing a long robe just like a Chinese immortal.

83. Saravati   cave 3

Saravati is the goddess of safety and fortune of states, she putting on a decoed hairpin crown, a colorful scarf and a skirt, just like a Chinese madame.

SPLENDID PAINTED SCULPTURES

1. Maitreya cross-leged

west   cave 275   Western Liang

It's the largest Maitreya statute of early-period still preserved. Behind the statute is a triangle nimbus. Buddha's crown on the head, silk towel with treasure ornaments and skirt. The craftsmanship is skillful. Beside it are two carved lions.

2. Maitreya in a niche

west   cave 268   Western Liang

In a round shaped niche, is a cross-leged Matreya whose head was repaired in Song dynasty. With a head of snaillike hair, the Buddha wearing a kasaya covering only a half of his body. Top of niche painted with lotus. Front: urna of Buddha, mural paints of bodhidattvas in both sides of it, flaming designs on door frame and Greek style pillar top.

3. Buddha in Dhyna   North Wei   cave 250

Buddha sits in meditation, tied up hair, square and large face. The modeling is free and easy.

4. Bodhisattva   cave 248   North Wei

A pretty bodhisattva, her expression is very dignified. No luxurious clothes. She looks smart and displays the beauty of the female. It was once repaired but the original form remained unchanged.

5. A group of painted sculptures

eastward niche   cave 432   North Wei

The niche is decoed with double-dragons and flame-nimbus designs. The main Buddha sits cross-leged, wearing a big sleeves robe. Two bodhisattvas were made out simple. Their expression are calm and peace, putting on crowns and skirts. The statute are colorful.

6. Kasyapa   south niche   cave 427   Sui dynasty

Kasyapa was one of great disciples of the Buddha. He was famous for his seriously ascetic practices. His hands forming a gesture of adoration in front of his breast, standing aside of the Buddha. He looks old and haggard yet his eyes are bright and smile still on his face.

7. Ananda   west niche   cave 427   Sui dynasty

Ananda was also a Buddha's dearest disciple. He was well known for his good memory. He also stands aside of the Buddha. Ananda looks well shaped. His clothes are simple and expression free and easy, just like a handsome young boy.

8. Kasyapa, bodhisattvas and lokapara

cave 322   Early Tang

Dasyapa looks health though haggard. He wears a piece of kasava and puts on a pair of monk's shoes. The budhisattva is high and thin, putting on a flower-shape crown and a long skirt. The lokapara in uniform with armour like a general. He is stepping on a demon in charge of local area.

9. Lokapara   cave 322   early Tang

It's a detail of above picture. He has big eyes and black eyebrow, his eyes are shining. Thick moustache and beard.

10. A group of painted sculptures

cave 45   High Tang

7 statutes in different shapes and characters. The main one sits seriously in the middle and looks kindly. Kasyapa is sophisticated, while Ananda looks young, clear and simple. The bodihisattva is pretty and the lokapara is mighty and friendship.

11. Ananda, bodhisattva and lokapara

south   cave 45   High Tang

A detail of the above picture. A young Ananda, a kindly bodhisattva and a friendship lokapara. But three statutes consist a harmonious whole.

12. Bodhisattva   north   cave 4354   High Tang

The statute's upper body naked with a lots of jewelled necklaces and strings of ornaments. She has tied up hair, slender eyebrows, red lips and thin body. She looks pretty and kind just like a pretty woman with blood and flesh.

13. Ananda   south   cave 45   High Tang

As a handsome young man, Ananda was a little disciple of the Buddha, his body turning round a little like a character of "s", his lips and eyebrows shows his youth and simple.

14. Vajrapani   south niche   cave 194   High Tang

This Vajrapani, with gripping two round eyes, open mouth, naked body, gripping hands. His well shaped muscles show us his strength.

15. Head of the great Buddha

cave 130   High Tang

The Buddha has a heigh of 26 meters in total, only its head over 7 meters, standing under the statute, a looker would feel the head smaller than it is. So the workers made the head comparatively longer.

16. Lokapara   north west   cave 46   High Tang

The Lokapara in armour is in anger. His limbs bends which show strength, in contrast the god in charge of local area is weak and incompetent.

17. Ananda, bodhisattva and lokapara

south   cave 159   Middle Tang

This is a rare piece of painting in ancient Tibetan regime. In the picture, young monk Ananda stands aside of the Buddha. The bodhisattva with a S shaped body and a square and well shaped face is pretty. Lokapara wears an armored uniform alike to a general of Tibetan army.

18. Kasyapas   1 cave 419   Sui dynasty
2 cave 45   High Tang

These two statutes were made in two different periods. The Sui style kasyapas looks like ascetic practicer. That made in High Tang like an old philosopher who had had rich expression of life.

19. Bodhisattva   south   cave 194   High Tang

With female beauty, this statute of male bodhisattva has a white face, and a well shaped body, his robe with various designs of flowers, a belt around his waist and silk towel on his two arms. One of rare artistic paintings in High Tang.

GORGEOUS SILK-PAINTINGS

1.   Bodhisattva as soul-guide

In purple mist, a male bodhisattva with female beauty, wearing luxurious clothes. One hand holding a small incencer burner, and the other lifting a color long banner. Stepping on a lotus, walking forward. A ghost of a woman in large robe after the bodhisattva. It is easy to read out the luxurious style of paintings in High Tang.

2. Avalokitesvara

A silk paint made in 910 A.D. The bodhisattva with bright eyes and small mouth and nose and large ears, wears a Buddha crown, luxurious ornaments in the body, her foot naked, putting on a skirt, her right hand holding a treasure bottle, the left hand grasping a branch of pillow. The picture is symmetric, clear and colorful with a distinct artistic style of Tang dynasty.

3. Ploughing, growing clothes and wedding ceremony

A picture showing the happiness in the Pure Land of Maitreya. A farmer in ploughing means get 7 if you gave 1, clothed handing on tree means trees would automatically growing clothes and a wedding ceremony means longevity of everyone and woman would be married at age of 500. It is in fact a picture of social life in Tang dynasty.

4. Tonsure of the men

Buddha Maitreya is preaching under a bodhitree. The king is ready to have his hair cut and to receive silas. An attendant holding a basin to contain cut hair standing aside and taking water to the king for clearing his body, 4 officials standing in humble. Horse and its driver in waiting for the king.

5. Tonsure of the women

A queen and several princess and concubines are also ready to be nuns. A nun is cutting the queen's hair, prince and others are standing in waiting. The color sedan on ground is usually used by the queen.

6. Story of Avalokitesvara-sutra

Main statute, with 6 arms, a male face, wears a Buddha crown, sitting cross-legged on a lotus stage. Among 6 arms, the upper two hands: the left holding a frog (sun), and the right one holding a three foot bird (moon), the below two hands, on the left: pure bottle, right: pears. A pictorial description of all kind of miseries: falling down from hill, being putting into jails, encounting with beasts, being killed, suffering from natural distress and fire.

7. Female donor and child

A part of the above picture. All of them are lay persons, the women seriously paying respect to the bodhisattva, the boy childishly stands aside.

8. Male donor

Also a detail of the 6th picture, front: an elder holding a hand stove; rear: a young man offering contributions to gods. Two persons kneeling down, they putting on small sleeves long robes, square towels on heads and belts around their waists. They are all painted as persons with individuality.

9. Head of male donor

The statute as a whole has been broken yet its head remains basically well. Judging from its craftsmanship, it belongs to a masterpiece. Square face, with black eyebrows, plain nose, shut mouth, long moustache and big ears, especially his eyes are bright. A square towel wrapped on his head makes the man more activate.

10. King's going out

Under the shade of umbrella, the king puts on a treasure crown, on his clothes there are signs of sun (three-foot—bird) and of moon (frog). Front of his breast is a green dragon. The left of below is a srivatsaloksana (swastilks). The right of below is unclear. Civil officials and generals are accompanying with the king. The modelling of persons are Hans and western minorities.

11. Buddha preaching the law

Under a bodhitree, the Buddha sits in a vajra seat surrounded by flowers, he wears a monastic kasaya. Bhiksus and bodhisattvas in both sides of him are listening to his teaching. Judging from its structure, color, modelling, it is really one masterpiece in Tang dynasty.

12. Story of Deer Daughter

Immortal in the south cave once pissed by a river, later a mother Dar have some water, then gave birth to the deer daughter. The deer daughter once asked the immortal in the north cave to lend her a kindling. From each of her foot prints grew a lotus flower. The picture is simple yet skillful.

13. Story of paradise of the Medician Buddha (section)

Three Buddhas standing side by side on a fenced stage. Middle: Buddha of medicine. His right hand grasping a pit of medicine, the left hand forming a gesture of promising. Left: attendant sun-light bodhisattva, hands holding lotus flower before his breast. A girl under the stage is praying for the Buddha.

14. The conception of the Buddha

Madam Maya fell asleep, she dreamed of a boy ridding an elephant from the sky and entering into her left waist. After the dream, she gave birth to Prince Siddhartha.

A wheel in clouds, a boy kneeling on the lotus seat in the back of an elephant and playing. Two attendant boys kneeling beside and looks very childish.

15. The washing of the new-born prince

Madam Maya gave birth to the prince under a no-wearing tree, there came 9 dragons to pull suitable hot water to wash him. In the picture, the baby well shaped standing in a basin on lotus flower. Maids offering help near him. The picture looks quite simple.

16. Dipamkara's prediction/prince's aware of four suffers of life

Above: Dipamkara is predicting for prince Siddhaarta.

Below: the prince travelling out of the city and seeing for the first time the aged, the sick and the dead. The sick on a bed, an old woman limping on road, a corpse lying on the top of a hill and his soul kneeling in sky. The distinct is the royal city.

17. Farewell in the mountain

The prince Siddhartha was decided give up secular life for ascetic one. He escaped in a midnight on the white horse and to distant mountains. His driver and the white horse were ready to back home. The prince gave all of his valuable things to the driver who were weeping. Even the hosse kneeling down and kissing the foot of the prince. A successful description of the feeling of one's departure from his good friends.

18. Lokapara

The Lokapara in anger, two hands holding swords, looks quite mighty. He wears a valuable cap and putting on around clothes. Two feet stepping on a crying god in charge of local area.

19. Vaistravana on his way across the water

An anger lokakpara, with a high hat, armored uniform, holding a JI (a weapon like spear), looks powerful and fiendish. Many deva generals follow him. What a magnificent landscape picture it is.

20. Vajrapani

An old aged Vajra, two hands holding vajra-nail, a naked body wearing only a piece of a towel. Well-shaped muscles show his strength and a kind of male beauty.

21. Vajrapani

This vajra's left hand's fingers holding together like a boxer, his right hand taking a stick. It's modelling is inferior to the former.

SIMPLE PAINTING ON BRICKS

1. Running Dragon

Discovered in a Temple of Laozhi in Mt. Dunhuang. Two running dragons on a model brick made in Five Dynasties. The dragons in a S shape, zigzaged bodies, is running and flying. It has a kind of beauty of simplicity.

2. Foreigner leading a camel

Excavated in Fuyei Temple, Dunhuang. The main Persian clothes is walking in desert, his one hand leading a camel, the other one holding a stick. The camel's raising its head and neck, so is its tail. Carrying a lot of goods, it walks slowly. The modelling is simple yet full of spirit of life.

ELEGANT AND FORCEFUL CALLIGRAPHIES

1. Official script: Mahaparinevana-sutra

The manuscript was written in Northern Wei. The words are square and fat. Vigorous and balanced brush stroke made it much valuable in the history.

2. Regular script: Buddhavatamsaka-sutra

Written in 513 A.D., it has a basically Wei style but also affected by official script tradition in Han dynasty.

3. Regular script: Mahaparinevana-sutra

It was written in 561 A.D. (northern Zhou). Basically, it has a regular style but influenced by traditional official and semi-cursive scripts. Words are all big and smooth showing a beauty of structure harmony.

4. Regular script: Fo shuo shen shen da hui xiang jing

The manuscript was written in 589 A.D. of Sui dynasty. The technique of writing is some over cautious. But they are full of strength and looks symmetric and vigorous.

5. Regular script: Fo shuo da yao shan qiao fang bian jing

All words on this piece of paper are very beautiful. They are square and balanced. Every stroke of words is clear and vigorous. It is an really elegant calligraphy. It could be regarded as a representative of writings in Tang dynasty.

6. Cursive hand: Za bao zang jing

The piece is regarded as a handwriting of a lecture report on Buddhism. Combination style of grass hand and running script. These words are all simple, free yet full of spirit and energy.